# The
# Lost Tribes
# of the
# Book of Mormon

# The
# Lost Tribes
# of the
# Book of Mormon

## The Rest of the Story

A correlation between the Nephite nation and the
Mound Builders of the eastern United States

by

# Phyllis Carol Olive

BONNEVILLE BOOKS
Springville, Utah

ISBN: 1-55517-575-9
v.1
Published by Bonneville Books
An imprint of Cedar Fort, Inc.
925 N. Main Springville, Utah, 84663
www.cedarfort.com

Distributed by:

Typeset by Marny K. Parkin
Cover design by Adam Ford
Cover design © 2001 by Lyle Mortimer
Cover painting by Phyllis Carol Olive

Printed in the United States of America
10 9 8 7 6 5 4 3 2 1
Printed on acid-free paper
Library of Congress Cataloging-in-Publication Data
Olive, Phyllis Carol.
The lost tribes of the Book of Mormon-- the rest of the story: a correlation between the Nephite nation and the mound builders of the Eastern United States/by Phyllis Carol Olive.
p. cm.
Includes bibliographical references.
ISBN 1-55517-575-9 (pbk. : alk. paper)
1. Lost tribes of Israel. 2. Mormon Church--Doctrines. I. Title.
BX8643.L66 .O55 2001
289.3'22--dc21
                    2001004406

# Acknowledgments

Scholars, archeologists, writers and the minds of many great men and women have contributed the wealth of knowledge that has helped me piece together this complicated puzzle. To them I owe a debt of gratitude, for I, without their past scholarship, could not have accomplished this work.

I would also like to recognize the talents of E. G. Squier, who took the time to draw the various earthen monuments found in the mound building region during his extensive explorations. His beautiful renderings, which were subsequently published in the Smithsonian, *Ancient Monuments of the Mississippi Valley,* in 1848, are worthy of view by an entire new generation. Thus, I have added as many as seemed appropriate to this body of work.

I also owe a debt of gratitude to my husband, Ron for his love and encouragement during the creation of this work and for the many times he proof read it for me. The editorial skills of my wonderful niece Judy Olin are also greatly appreciated as is the encouragement given me by my entire family.

Neither can I neglect to give recognition to the influence of the Holy Spirit during the creation process. I simply could not have done it alone.

# Contents

Michigan Relic depicting Ark of the Covenant.
Photo, Wayne May, *Ancient American Magazine.*

# Preface

In the introduction to the Book of Mormon we read of the Angel Moroni's visit to Joseph Smith, and the instructions he was given by that heavenly messenger in bringing forth the Book of Mormon. He was told, among other things,

> there was a book deposited, written upon gold plates, giving an account of the former inhabitants of this continent, and the source from whence they sprang. He also said that the fulness of the everlasting Gospel was contained in it, as delivered by the Savior to the ancient inhabitants.

Concerning the contents of the book we read:

> Wherefore, it is an abridgment of the record of the people of Nephi, and also of the Lamanites-Written to the Lamanites, who are a remnant of the house of Israel; and also to Jew and Gentile-Written by way of commandment, and also by the spirit of prophecy and of revelation-Written and sealed up, and hid up unto the Lord, that they might not be destroyed-To come forth by the gift and power of God unto the interpretation thereof-Sealed by the hand of

Moroni, and hid up unto the Lord, to come forth in due time by way of the Gentile-The interpretation thereof by the gift of God.

An abridgment taken from the Book of Ether also, which is a record of the people of Jared, who were scattered at the time the Lord confounded the language of the people, when they were building a tower to get to heaven-Which is to show unto the remnant of the House of Israel what great things the Lord hath done for their fathers; and that they may know the covenants of the Lord, that they are not cast off forever- And also to the convincing of the Jew and Gentile that JESUS is the CHRIST, the ETERNAL GOD, manifesting himself unto all nations-And now, if there are faults they are the mistakes of men; wherefore, condemn not the things of God, that ye may be found spotless at the judgment-seat of Christ. (Title page, Book of Mormon)

That ancient record was subsequently published in 1830 as the Book of Mormon. It has gone forth into the world in this last and final dispensation to act as a second witness of Jesus Christ and verifies to mankind that God speaks to people in all lands and in all dispensations of time. The message of hope and salvation found within its pages has brought countless souls into the fold and will yet speak to the honest in heart until the end of time.

~   ~   ~

By heavenly design, the Holy Ghost will act as testifier to the truthfulness of this sacred record. Thus, physical evidence of its authenticity has not been necessary. Nevertheless, men's natural curiosity has led many in search of the lost lands of the Book of Mormon, only to have it elude them these many years. Fortunately, the various geographical descriptions found within the text itself will ultimately lead us to the lands we seek.

Descriptive clues are interspersed throughout the entire Book of Mormon, one of which informs us that the promised land was a land destined for great and marvelous things. In 1 Nephi 13:13–20 we read of the prophetic future of the land of promise and the formation of the great latter-day nation known as the United States of America.

> And it came to pass that I beheld the Spirit of God, that it wrought upon other Gentiles; and they went forth out of captivity, upon the many waters.
>
> And it came to pass that I beheld many multitudes of the Gentiles upon the land of promise; and I beheld the wrath of God, that it was upon the seed of my brethren; and they were scattered before the Gentiles and were smitten.
>
> And I beheld the Spirit of the Lord, that it was upon the Gentiles, and they did prosper and obtain the land for their inheritance; and I beheld that they were white, and exceedingly fair and beautiful, like unto my people before they were slain.
>
> And it came to pass that I, Nephi, beheld that the Gentiles who had gone forth out of captivity did humble themselves before the Lord; and the power of the Lord was with them.
>
> And I beheld that their mother Gentiles were gathered together upon the waters, and upon the land also, to battle against them.
>
> And I beheld that the power of God was with them, and also that the wrath of God was upon all those that were gathered together against them to battle.
>
> And I, Nephi, beheld that the Gentiles that had gone out of captivity were delivered by the power of God out of the hands of all other nations.
>
> And it came to pass that I, Nephi, beheld that they did prosper in the land; and I beheld a book, and it was carried forth among them. (1 Ne. 13:13–20)

These scriptures clearly indicate the land of promise was destined to be a refuge for the peoples of the world; a land of liberty, and, as still other scriptures inform us, the place of the New Jerusalem. Moreover, it was a place where a government could be set up that would prepare the way for the restitution of all things. Ezra Taft Benson bears further witness of this nation's divine origins:

> I bear witness that America's history was foreknown to God; that His divine intervention and merciful providence has given us both peace and prosperity in this beloved land; that through His omniscience and benevolent design He selected and sent some of His choicest spirits to lay the foundation of our government (see *D&C* 101:80). These men were inspired of God to do the work they accomplished. They were not evil men. Their work was a prologue to the restoration of the gospel and the Church of Jesus Christ. It was done in fulfillment of the ancient prophets who declared this was a promised land, a land of liberty unto the Gentiles, and that is us. (*Teachings of Ezra Taft Benson*, 575–76)

By this and various other scriptures, it appears that America the beautiful was the land "choice above all others" spoken of by the prophets. Consequently, the American Indians must be the remnants of those whose history is contained in that sacred work. From President James R. Clark in a message from the First Presidency we read:

> The Book of Mormon is a record of the forefathers of our western tribes of Indians; having been found through the ministration of an holy angel, and translated into our own language by the gift and power of God, after having been hid up in the earth for the last fourteen hundred years, containing the word of God which was delivered unto them. By it we learn that our western tribes of Indians are descendants from that Joseph which was sold into Egypt, and that the land of America is a promised land unto them, and unto it all the tribes of Israel will come, with as many of the gentiles as shall comply with the requisitions of the new covenant. But the tribe of Judah will return to old Jerusalem. The city of Zion spoken of by David, in the one hundred and second Psalm, will be built upon the land of America, "And the ransomed of the Lord shall return, and come to Zion with songs and everlasting joy upon their

heads. (James R. Clark, *Messages from the First Presidency,* 6:103)

This land, choice above all others, was kept hidden from all nations and was held in reserve by the power of God to be a land of liberty to those whom God would ultimately lead to her shores. Since neither the lands to the north or the south of the United States enjoy the fulness of those blessings promised those who inhabit the promised land, we must look to the United States of America for placement of the Book of Mormon lands. And, what better place to start than those territories in the vicinity of the only known landmark we have, the beautiful Hill Cumorah in New York state?

A more comprehensive study of those limited regions that made up the lands of the Nephites and Jaredites is found in this author's *The Lost Lands of the Book of Mormon.* How that limited territory fits into the over-all mound building regions, however, is equally interesting, for the entire country, indeed the entire hemisphere was involved in that ancient drama. Thus, from the archeological findings that surfaced while researching the first book, this book evolved.

The acquisition of facts over the centuries, regardless of the debates and controversies that surfaced along the way, play a big part in proving the whereabouts of those whose history is contained in the Book of Mormon. Thus, this work will cover the evolutionary process of scientific thought from those made during the early days of colonization to those made in the last century, with the descriptions given in the Book of Mormon as the missing pieces of the puzzle.

~ ~ ~

Chapter One

# Ancient Monuments

It has long been known that the eastern United States was once populated by an ancient people. Yet for some unknown reason, this territory, filled with literally tens of thousands of earthen monuments and impressive mounds, has all too often been disregarded in the search for the lost lands of the Book of Mormon. This is due, in part, to the fact the archeological world itself cannot decide on just who it was that built these ancient works and why their builders mysteriously disappeared around 400 A.D. In fact, that single subject has been a source of controversy and conjecture for the last three centuries. Yet, with the inclusion of just one more piece of the puzzle, the ancient records of the Nephites and Jaredites, that mystery could have been cleared up long ago, for the Book of Mormon contains the answers so many seek.

All too often science and religion are at odds with one another. But, in this instance, the archeological findings of the past centuries do much in helping us locate the lost lands of the Nephites and Jaredites. In fact, so much information has been gleaned over the years that we can now say, without hesitation, that nowhere else on earth is better suited to be the lands described within the Book of Mormon than the eastern United States.

The ancient monuments built up by those whose history is contained in the scriptures are scattered across the entire eastern third of the country. Mounds and impressive earthen enclosures rise high above the surrounding landscape and stand in mute silence over a land that once heard the bustling sounds of busy settlements and prosperous cities. Sadly, a region all but forgotten. So little attention is paid the mound building regions today that few of this generation have even heard of it, let alone the impressive artifacts scattered throughout the territory.

~ ~ ~

The remains of splendid stone palaces and temples found in countries around the world leave indisputable evidence of the magnificent empires that once occupied those lands. Unfortunately, the territory of the modern-day United States has few such spectacular monuments, for those found in this country were made of wood and earth, and, since wood decays, not much has survived the ages. Even this small piece of information is important, however, for those familiar with the Book of Mormon will recall that both the Nephites and Jaredites built their temples and cities with wood. Thus, the ancient works found in the eastern portion of the United States match more closely those cities and temples described in the scriptures than those made of stone in the more southern regions of the Hemisphere.

The scriptures themselves reaffirm this supposition, for they inform us the early Nephite colonists learned the art of working in wood under the watchful eye of Nephi, who taught them many things, including how to construct their buildings.

> And I did teach my people to build buildings, and to
> work in all manner of wood, and of iron, and of copper, and
> of brass, and of steel, and of gold, and of silver, and of pre-
> cious ores, which were in great abundance. (2 Ne. 5:15)

Again we read:

> And we multiplied exceedingly, and spread upon the
> face of the land, and became exceedingly rich in gold, and
> in silver, and in precious things, and in fine workmanship of
> wood, in buildings, and in machinery, and also in iron and
> copper, and brass and steel, making all manner of tools of
> every kind to till the ground, and weapons of war-yea, the
> sharp pointed arrow, and the quiver, and the dart, and the
> javelin, and all preparations for war. (Jarom 1:8)

At no time do we read they learned the art of working in
stone or that they even needed to, for they resided in one of the
richest timberlands in the world. There was absolutely no need
to resort to the burdensome task of building in stone—even
when the forests were temporarily depleted, for when their
local trees were all used up they simply shipped more in from
other areas.

> And it came to pass as timber was exceedingly scarce
> in the land northward, they did send forth much by the way
> of shipping. (Hel. 3:10)

We might remember that the Nephites faced just such a
problem when they migrated northward and came upon a land
that was nearly barren of trees. Apparently the former inhabitants, the Jaredites, also built with wood and had carelessly
stripped the land of her vast forest growth just prior to the
Nephites entrance into the region. Thus, the Nephites simply
lived in tents and built their homes with cement for a time,
until the trees grew back again.

> Yea, and they did spread forth unto all parts of the
> land into whatever parts it had not been rendered desolate
> and without timber, because of the many inhabitants who
> had before inherited the land. . . .

3

And the people who were in the land northward did dwell in tents, and in houses of cement, and they did suffer whatsoever tree should spring up upon the face of the land that it should grow up, that in time they might have timber to build their houses, yea, their cities, and their temples, and their synagogues, and their sanctuaries, and all manner of their buildings. (Hel. 3:5, 9)

These scriptures make it abundantly clear that both the Nephites and Jaredites worked primarily in wood. Unfortunately, wood decays, especially in such a moist environment, therefore, only the faintest hint of any wooden structure would survive the centuries. We should also remember that the greater portion of both the Nephite and Jaredite civilizations were burned to the ground at the end of their respective eras. The Jaredite record of that terrible time was carefully recorded by Ether who noted the loss of both lives and property.

Now the name of the brother of Lib was called Shiz. And it came to pass that Shiz pursued after Coriantumr, and he did overthrow many cities, and he did slay both women and children, and he did burn the cities. (Ether 14:17)

Likewise, during the Nephite era, the Lamanites burned each city they came to as they mercilessly drove the Nephites to their final stand around the Hill Cumorah.

And it came to pass that whatsoever lands we had passed by, and the inhabitants thereof were not gathered in, were destroyed by the Lamanites, and their towns, and villages, and cities were burned with fire; and thus three hundred and seventy and nine years passed away. (Morm. 5:5)

These scriptures clarify why so little of either civilization endured the ages, for only the earthen walls and enclosures surrounding their towns and villages could have survived such terrible conflagrations.

What little remained of those ancient cities would naturally pale in comparison to the grand stone ruins found in Central and South America. Thus, they tend to be overlooked in our search for the lost lands of the Book of Mormon. Nevertheless, since the scriptures clearly indicate that both the Nephites and Jaredites built their cities with wood, including their temples and synagogues, we have a major correlation between those civilizations once occupying the eastern woodlands and those mentioned in the Book of Mormon. Moreover, because these materials are highly perishable, and because so many were destroyed by fire, we also have a clue as to why the lands of the Book of Mormon have remained hidden for such a long time, for little of that ancient time survived to tell the story.

Fortunately, many of their towns and cities were surrounded by great earthen enclosures which were not destroyed. Thus, evidence of that distant era is still scattered across the entire eastern third of the country. The significance of such impressive monuments is of little interest to modern-day America, however, who seem to know more about the remnants of those grand civilizations in Central and Southern America than the heritage in their own back yards. Thus, a people lost through time have remained so.

> An ancient and unknown people left remains of settled life, and of a certain degree of civilization, in the valleys of the Mississippi and it tributaries. We have no authentic name for them either as a nation or a race; therefore they are called "Mound-Builders," this name having been suggested by an important class of their works.[1]

~  ~  ~

Because centuries of dense forestation eventually covered the abandoned mound centers, the eastern woodlands were filled with mystery when the white man first entered the region. It took years to discover the magnitude of the Mound Builder's territory and the wonderful treasures hidden away in their burial sites. Silverberg, author of *The Mound Builders,* describes that early scene:

> The mounds lacked beauty and elegance, perhaps.
> They were mere heaps of earth. Some were colossal, like
> the Cahokia Mound in Illinois, 100 feet high and covering
> 16 acres; others were mere blisters rising from the earth.
> Some stood in solitary grandeur above broad plains, while
> others sprouted in thick colonies. All were overgrown with
> trees and shrubbery, so that their outlines could barely be
> distinguished, although, once cleared, the mounds revealed
> their artificial nature by their regularity and symmetry of
> shape. Within many of them were human bones, weapons,
> tools, jewelry.[2]

These impressive earthen monuments were first recorded by de Soto and his men in 1539, when they reached the shores of Florida in search of kingdoms as rich as those found in Peru and Central America. Although it soon became apparent there were simply none to be found, they continued to search for a fabled "city of gold," finding instead only numerous mounds with mystery shrouded origins.

French colonists who landed in 1562, were the next to enter the picture and they, too, came across these strange earthen monuments. Fortunately, they were careful to record their finds, and even drew pictures of some in an effort to preserve a record for succeeding generations.

From the records of a Frenchman who lived among the Indians from 1698 to 1732, we gain our first indications of the purpose for some of the mounds. He recorded: "The chief's house stood upon a mound of earth about eight feet high and sixty feet across,"[3] indicating that some, at least, were simply residential platforms for the elite.

While a few mounds found in the south were still being used by local tribes when the French first began to explore the region in the seventeenth century, the earthen works in the north had long been abandoned and were covered with so much vegetation they appeared like nothing more than natural formations. As explorers moved further northward, however, it soon became apparent they were not natural formations at all

Cluster of mounds.
Madaillac, *Pre-Historic America,* 1893.

but were man made structures. Moreover, they soon discovered the entire eastern woodlands were simply dotted with them.

Although these earthen monuments were discovered throughout the territory, a great number were found along the great fathers of waters, the Mississippi. This expansive region has a "total drainage area of close to 1,250,000 square miles, an area equal in size to the country of India. Its length is almost equal to that of the 4,000 mile Amazon River which lies near the equator and flows through dense tropical forests."[4]

L. N. Shaffer, in *Native Americans before 1492,* describes this choice region further:

> Eastern North America's moundbuilding region is the only one in the hemisphere where the location of large centers was so closely related to a network of rivers. None of the great civilizations in Mesoamerica and the Andes was so closely identified with a large river-basin. They generally had their origins in tropical or subtropical climates where the land rises steeply from coastal lowlands to high mountain plateau, and much of the terrain is marked by numerous narrow and relatively steep drainage basins. Such local, climate growing conditions, and resources vary considerably from one elevation to another, and, in general, the easiest exchange networks and political structures brought about a vertical integration of lowland with highland.

Thus, it is only the mound building regions of Eastern North American that resembles the pattern of eastern Hemisphere, where early civilizations were closely identified with rivers; the Tigris-Euphrates, the Nile, the Indus, and the Yellow River in China. Like the Mississippi, these rivers are located in temperate latitude, between 30 and 40 degrees north of the equator. There are, however, significant differences between the locales of these early riverine civilizations of Africa and India and Eastern North America's moundbuilding region. One is that relatively steady and moderate amount of rain reliably falls over the Eastern Woodlands, whereas the Tigris-Euphrates, the Nile, the Indus, and the Yellow rivers flow for most of their courses through arid lands, in some cases through deserts and in others through what were once grasslands. Most of their water supply comes from the mountains where their headwaters are located far from the coasts.[5]

It is no wonder the scriptures refer to the promised land as "a land choice above all others."

> And inasmuch as ye shall keep my commandments ye shall prosper and shall be led to a land of promise; yea a land which I have prepared for you; yea a land which is choice above all others. (1 Ne. 2:20)

Because of the numerous waterways that flow through the countryside and the amount of annual rainfall, the North American woodlands have always been very dense, so dense, in fact, they were often referred to as "primeval forests" by early explorers.

> The great age of these mounds and inclosures is shown by their relation to the primeval forests in which most of them were discovered. I say primeval forests, because they seemed primeval to the first white men who explored them. Of course there were no unbroken forests at such points in the Ohio Valley, for instance, while they were occupied by the Mound-Builders, who were settled agricultural people, whose civilized industry is attested by their remains. If they found forests in the valleys they occupied,

these were cleared away to make room for their towns, inclosures, mounds, and cultivated fields; and when, after many ages of such occupation, they finally left, or were driven away, a long period must have elapsed before the trees began to grow freely in and around their abandoned works. Moreover, observation shows that the trees which first make their appearance in such deserted places are not regular forest trees. The beginning of such growths as will cover them with great forests comes later, when other preliminary growths have appeared and gone to decay.[6]

From all historical accounts, the mound building region has always been rich in natural resources. Early travelers reported seeing an infinite variety of animals such as deer, wild turkey, beaver and other small creatures. Birds were reported to have flown over the area in such thick flocks they actually darkened the sky, and fish were said to have been so large they threatened to overturn their boats. The woodlands could easily have provided all the necessities of life for those living in the region. Those living near the Great Lakes, for instance, "were using 275 species of plants for medicine, 130 species for food, 31 species as magical charms, 27 species for smoking, and 25 species as dyes and various utilitarian purpose." At sites such a Lamoka Lake in New York, "the people fed on 28 species of mammals, 13 species of birds, turtles, and at least 5 species of fish, in addition to a substantial amount of native plant food."[7] It is easy to see why this fruitful region was the most populated area north of Mexico before European contact.

~ ~ ~

As immigrants began to flood the promised land in fulfillment of prophecy in the eighteenth and nineteenth centuries, most mounds were safely outside the occupied regions of the new republic, which was still restricted to the eastern seaboard. However, as colonists began to pour over the Appalachian Mountain range in search of new territories, and

9

Mound at Miamisburg, Ohio, 65 ft. high.
Photo, Wayne May, *Ancient American Magazine.*

forests began to fall in preparation for towns and cities, mounds that had long been hidden by centuries of forest growth began to emerge from their hiding places. Staggering numbers were found. Bones, too, were found; so old they crumbled at the touch, and artifacts, which showed evidence of great antiquity, were found by the basket loads. It seemed that every farmer who plowed his land came up with some small piece of evidence that an ancient civilization once occupied the region.

As time passed and settlers entered the Ohio Valley, the prevailing notion that a vanished race once lived in the territory began to gain in popularity, for literally thousands of mysterious mounds were found throughout the region. Ten thousand were found in Ohio alone. Most were located south of the Great Lakes with the northern mound zone beginning in western New York. All were located west of the Appalachian Mountains except those located in the southeast-the Carolinas, Georgia, Alabama and Florida. Their size and shapes varied with the location. The mounds along the Great Lakes, for example, remained rather low, usually no more than three or four feet high, and

Great Serpent Mound.
Courtesy Museum of the American Indian, Smithsonian Institution. N21598.

took the form of huge birds, reptiles, various animals, and even men. In Ohio the shape was usually conical, and in the lower Mississippi the flat topped pyramid predominated.

Europeans and Americans alike were amazed by these incredible monuments, yet when the local natives were asked about their origins they were told they had "belonged to the ancestors of the Native Americans . . . when they had large towns and had been as numerous as trees in the woods." This rather primitive estimate actually may have not been far off, for in 1983, Henry F. Dobyns published an estimate that as many as eighteen million people may have occupied the territory in ancient times. Although that number remains controversial, other estimates are climbing upward toward that mark, with one estimating seven million and another twelve.[9] Or, as the Book of Mormon tells us, "they were as numerous as the hosts of Israel" (Mosiah 8:8).

~ ~ ~

As explorations of the eastern woodlands continued, first hand accounts of their findings began to appear in print, including tales of various Indian tribes discovered throughout the region. As interesting as these stories were, however, the general populace found those articles about the numerous mounds and strange pyramidal structures scattered all across the countryside of even greater interest. As more and more was written on the subject, the public soon found themselves caught up in what we might call "mound fever." Unfortunately, the added publicity brought growing numbers of amateur archeologists into the field, and ancient monuments began to disappear by the thousands as shovels and hoes shaved down the mounds and men dug deep in search of ancient treasures. Thus, those magnificent works that had long withstood the winds of time were slowly disappearing, and, along with them, the historical evidence of a noble race lost through time.

As the mounds began to disappear, more and more fantastic stories of lost races and vanished empires began to surface. Amazing stories had already circulated about the fabulous wealth and great kingdoms found in Central and South America, and early colonists had high hopes of coming across some evidence of a great romantic past in North America as well. Unfortunately, they found only great expansive forests and broad plains occupied by a naked and savage people whose origin was the only question holding much intrigue. To the early colonists the Indians appeared to be nothing more than simple hunter-gatherers, and offered no evidence of any vanished greatness. Consequently, they continued to believe a more exotic "lost race" built the mounds. Little did they know of the grandeur these people once attained during the height of the Nephite era or the vast civilization that once spread across the land. Fortunately, one lone book, the Book of Mormon, tells us of their former greatness; unfortunately, a book little read by those who inquire after the early beginnings of the Native American people.

~ ~ ~

## Notes

1. Baldwin, *Ancient America,* 17.
2. Silverburg, *Mound Builders,* 10.
3. Ibid., 27.
4. Shaffer, *Native Americans before 1492,* introduction, 10.
5. Ibid., 10–11.
6. Baldwin, *Ancient America,* 51.
7. Shaffer, *Native Americans before 1492,* 18.
8. Ibid., 4.
9. Ibid.

Chapter Two

# Legends, Myths, and Truths

In 1796, Francis Baily accompanied a party of settlers down the Ohio River and discovered numerous earthen monuments. So impressive were they that Baily wrote:

> The mounds must have been "built by a race of people more enlightened than the present Indians, and at some period of time very far distant; for the present Indians know nothing about their use, nor have they any tradition concerning them.[1]

Such comments about their great antiquity continued to fuel the fire of speculation regarding the origin of the mounds, and more and more books on the subject began to pop up everywhere. Even so, it soon became apparent that no one had even the slightest idea of who built them or why those who did ultimately disappeared.

To the influx of settlers in the New World the mounds were simply "a nuisance," and were often plowed down to prepare their newly acquired lands for cultivation. To antiquarians,

15

however, they were remnants of a lost race, ones that needed extensive investigation. Thus, as more and more mounds began to be excavated, and artifacts discovered, the supposed myth of a "lost race" took hold and began to gain in popularity.

Numerous theories surfaced over the years, each unique in some respect, yet each containing similarities and each seemingly grounded in fact. Early explorers were so convinced the mounds could not have been built by local savages that they attributed them to Vikings, Romans, Phoenicians or any number of other ancient mariners; anyone other than the Native American Indians, for surely they were far too primitive to have erected such wonderful works. Others, on the other hand, were just as convinced the forerunners of the Native Americans did build the mounds and suggested they were simply a more enlightened race at some earlier period in time. (Little did they know how right they were!)

It is difficult to explain the great amount of interest given mound exploration in the eighteenth and nineteenth centuries. From the common digs by amateur archeologists to more scientific expeditions by government agencies, the origin of the Mound Builders and their treasures were a favorite topic of conversation among both lay people and those from the scholastic world as well. The controversy regarding whether the Mound Builders were a "lost race" or simply the ancestors of the modern Indians raged on in both print and discussions decade after decade. It was almost like a war was in progress with each side anxiously trying to persuade the opposing side to their way of thinking. Sometimes this happened, but often new evidence surfaced which caused many to pull right back to their original way of thinking. Thus, the controversy raged on and on and on.

Theories abounded, with each more fantastic than the first. Both serious books and popular novels had the Mound Builders sailing to North America from the lost continent of Atlantis or from various other eastern or Asiatic countries.

Others postulated they came across the Baring Straits and then slowly migrated eastward while still others suggested they migrated northward from the southern and central portions of the hemisphere.

~ ~ ~

Now, the origin of the "Red Man" was just as big a mystery as the mounds, and had been since their discovery at the time of European contact. Consequently, speculation about that subject continued as well. However, one theory more than any other prevailed during the eighteenth and nineteenth centuries— the theory that the North American Indians were descended from the Lost Tribes of Israel—those that had been led away captive by the Assyrians and were never heard from again. Moreover, it seemed there were so many similarities between the Hebrews and the Native Americans that no one could totally discount that possibility. Thus, many of that day were perfectly comfortable with the notion that the mounds were built by none other than the Ten Lost Tribes themselves.

As a recap of those events leading up to the captivity and ultimate dispersion of Israel, we might remember that after the twelve sons of Jacob, (son of Isaac and grandson of Abraham) had been established as a nation, the various tribes began to dabble in the same idolatrous practices as neighboring regions— including human sacrifice. Needless to say this pained the Lord greatly, for it was he who led their forefathers out of bondage and, after many miracles on their behalf, established them as nation. Even so, the Lord gave them every chance for repentance. Unfortunately, they refused. Nevertheless, in an effort to preserve them from utter destruction, he ultimately allowed their enemies to carry them off captive.

The Bible informs us that the nation of Israel was divided at this point in history, for ten of the tribes withdrew from their brethren and set up an entirely separate kingdom further to the north. Unfortunately, both kingdoms were eventually overthrown and all twelve tribes were carried away captive. That terrible episode in history was one of the darkest ever recorded and will not be addressed at this time. But in short, those occupying the southern kingdom were eventually allowed to return, while those from the northern kingdom were never heard from again. Unfortunately, the scriptures are completely silent on where they might be. Thus, they have ever after been referred to as "the Ten Lost Tribes of Israel." The only hint we have of their whereabouts comes to us from the apocrypha, which indicates they eventually journeyed northward, crossing the great River Euphrates and heading for a land never before inhabited by man. Such accounts led many of the eighteenth and nineteenth century to believe their ultimate destination was the North American Continent and that the North American Indians, so like the Hebrews in so many ways, were none other than the ten lost tribes themselves.

Since the Indians themselves made it known to James Adair that the nation from which they sprang were all of one color, the theory that the Indians had a unified national origin such as that of Israel continued to thrive. Yet, not all were willing to go that far. Atwater, a noted authority on the American Indians, speculated that the Indians did not necessarily descend from Israel, but were more likely descended from a non-Indian race that was similar in culture to the Hebrews of Palestine. Thus, the origins of the Red Man provided as much intrigue as the controversy surrounding the mounds and the various treasures interred within them.

In the continuing debate on the matter, many notable writers began to speculate that the "'high places'" of the Israelites were similar to the mounds in the northeastern United States. In 2 Kings 17:10–11, we read, "And they set them up images and groves in every high hill, and under every green tree; And there they burnt incense in all the high places, as did the heathen." Because of this, and numerous other similarities, many who equated the mounds with the "high places" of Israel, continued to foster the belief that the Indians had an Israelitish background. Atwater commented on that very subject:

> On the high places of Palestine great national affairs were transacted. Here they crowned and deposed their kings; here they concluded peace and declared war. Here the nation assembled at stated seasons, to perform the solemn worship of their deities. Here they celebrated anniversaries of great national events. . . . Let the reader examine the mounds of Ohio, and then ask himself, whether those who raised our monuments, were not originally from Asia . . . examine the loftiest mounds (in Ohio) and then compare them with those described as being in Palestine.[2]

Thus, the theory that the Indians were descendants of the Lost Tribes of Israel continued to flourish.

~ ~ ~

Of great importance in proving an Israelitish origin for the Native Americans is the fact that most Indian tribes worshiped only one supreme God. Now this fact is of no small importance in such a pursuit, for Israel had been commanded to have no other Gods before them.

Josiah Priest, commenting on Mr. Adair's knowledge of the matter had this to say:

> Mr. Adair is very full in this, "that the Indians have but one God, the great Yohewah, whom they call the great, beneficent supreme and holy Spirit, who dwells above the clouds, and who dwells with good people, and is the only object of worship." So different are they from all the idolatrous heathen upon earth. He assures that they hold this great divine Spirit as the immediate head of their community; which opinion he conceives they must have derived from the ancient theocracy in Israel. He assures that the Indians are intoxicated with religious pride, and call all other people the accursed people; and have time out of mind been accustomed to hold them in great contempt. Their ancestors they boast to have been under the immediate government of Yohewah, who was with them, and directed

them by his prophets, while the rest of the world were out-
laws, pleased themselves, with the idea that God has chosen
them from the rest of mankind as his peculiar people and of
viewing themselves hated by all men. These things show
that they acknowledge but one God. [3]

(So often in past generations those from Israel have got-
ten themselves into trouble with their Gentile neighbors with
such lofty remarks. Interestingly, so did the Zoramites in the
Book of Mormon.)

Even though their worship of God had become distorted
over the years, the Indian's reverence for that Supreme Being
has remained universal among most. Josiah Priest's comments
on that subject are enlightening.

But little short of three hundred thousand gods have
existed in the bewildered imaginations of the pagan world.
Every thing, almost, has been deified by the heathen. Not
liking to retain God in their knowledge, and professing
themselves to be wise, they became fools; and they changed
the glory of the one living God into images and beast, birds,
reptiles, and creeping things. There has been the most
astonishing inclination in the world of mankind to do thus.
But there is a new world of savages, chiefly if not wholly,
free from such wild idolatry. Doctor Boudinot (being
assured by many good witnesses,) says of the Indians who
have been known in his day; "They were never known
(whatever mercenary Spanish writers may have written to
the contrary) to pay the least adoration to images or dead
persons to celestial luminaries, to evil spirits, or to any created beings whatever." Mr. Adair says the same, and assures
that "not one of the numerous tribes and nations, from Hud-
son's Bay to the Mississippi, have ever been known to
attempt the formation of any image of God." Du Pratz was
very intimate with the chief of those Indians called "the
Guardian of the Temple," near the Mississippi. He inquired
of them the nature of their worship. The chief informed him
they worshiped the great and most perfect spirit; and said.
"He is so great and powerful that in comparison with him
all others are as nothing. He made all things that we see, and

all things that we cannot see." The chief went on to speak of God as having made little spirits, called free servants, who always stand before the Great Spirit ready to do his will.[4]

Students of the Book of Mormon will remember the account of the missionary efforts of the Nephites to the Lamanites (Indians), in the Book of Mormon. As that story unfolds, one of the sons of Mosiah asked the king of the Lamanites if he believed in God. He, in turn, inquired if God were the Great Spirit.

> And the king said: Is God that Great Spirit that brought our fathers out of the land of Jerusalem? And Aaron said unto him: yea, he is that Great Spirit and he created all things both in heaven and in earth. Believest thou this?
>
> And he said: yea, I believe that the Great Spirit created all things, and I desire that ye should tell me concerning all these things, and I will believe thy words. (Alma 22:9–11)

These latter-day scriptures make it abundantly clear that even the earliest inhabitants of America had been familiar with the Great Spirit. Mr. Hebard, a settled minister gives us his opinion on the matter:

> Let this fact of the Indians generally adhering to one, and only one God, be contrasted with the polytheism of the world of pagans, and heathen besides; with the idle and ridiculous notions of heathen gods and goddesses; and who can doubt of the true origin of the natives of our continent? They are fatally destitute of proper view of God and religion. But they have brought down by tradition from their remote ancestors, the notion of there being but one great and true God; which affords a most substantial argument in favor of their being the ancient Israel.[5]

Even those far to the west believed in one Great Spirit. Lewis and Clark recorded, "the whole religion of the Mandans consists in a belief of one Great Spirit presiding over their destinies."[6]

Since the Indians have no written language, much of our knowledge of their history comes to us from legends carefully preserved in the memories of special members of each tribe. Such care is given the transfer of legends from generation to generation that we must give some measure of credence to those that have survived the years. One such legends reveals that, "once the waters had overflowed all the land and drowned all people then living, except a few who made a great canoe and were saved."₇ Another reveals that, "A long time ago the people went to build a high place; that while they were building, they lost their language, and could not understand each other."

Still another legend recounted by a tribe who had never before seen white men, tells that a great while ago they had a common father who had the other people under him. He had twelve sons by whom he administered his government; but because the sons behaved illy, they lost this government.₈ Such similarities to the family of the ancient Patriarch Jacob and his twelve sons, which ultimately became the tribes of Israel, cannot be dismissed easily. Neither can it be dismissed that many Hebrew customs and traits can also be found in Indian cultures. In his early work, *History of the North American Indians,* James Adair suggests a number of similarities, including the fact the Indians are divided into tribes just as Israel had been.

Adair's impressive work was written in 1775, and his many years as an English trader among the Indians (1735 to 1775), gave him insights into their lives not previously understood. After years of studying their cultures he was of the decided opinion that there were numerous similarities between the Indians and the Hebrew people. Not surprisingly, these conclusion, which incorporated a great portion of his book, helped to perpetuate the theory that the Mound Builders were truly the Ten Lost Tribes themselves.

In addressing the growing body of evidence that the Indians had Israelite origins, Josiah Priest, in his own work, *Wonders of Nature and Providence* (1825), enumerates on many, including those of Adairs. He commented that even their feasts were similar to Israel's, such as those that resemble the feast of the Passover, the feast of harvest, and the annual expiation of sin. He further informs us that during these feasts they dance and sing and have words such as Hallelujah and Yohewah in the syllables which compose the words. He went on to say, "The Indians have their feasts of first ripe fruits, or of green corn; and will eat none of their corn till a part is thus given to God." He further commented, "The celebrated Penn, Mr. Adair, and Col. Smith, with others, unite in these testimonies."[9]

He recounts a number of other traditions as well, such as the fact that they sacrifice before going to war and afterwards, and, if they were victorious, they have their religious dance. They have a high priest, whom they reverence, and they believe in an afterlife with ultimate rewards and punishments. They have their imitation of the ark of the covenant as well as a tribe resembling the tribe of Levi. Moreover, it is believed they have a city of refuge just as ancient Israel had. And the list goes on and on.

Now, even though many of their traditions have been obviously distorted and broken over the centuries, there seems to be a significant body of evidence that the Indians have Israelite origins. Adair believed further that even their reckoning of time is the same as the Hebrew, for they begin their year, as did Israel, at the first appearance of the new moon after the vernal equinox. They reckon by the four seasons, and by the subdivision of the moons.[10] Thus, far too many things fit far too comfortably with the probability of their having Israelitish origins than can be reconciled with any other explanation.

Interestingly, people in many different countries agreed with that assumption. "It was ascertained in the *Star in the West*, that Spaniards, Portuguese, French, English, Jews, and Christians, men of learning, and the illiterate, and sea-faring men; all have united in the statements of facts, which go to indicate that these Indians are the descendants of Israel!"[11]

Josiah Priest, author, archeologist, poet and a prolific writer of his time, wrote in 1825:

> It is again asked, is it possible to find another people on earth exhibiting an equal degree of evidence of their being the ten tribes of Israel? Can another people on earth be found exhibiting one sixth part of the evidence adduced in favour of the American Natives?... Our aborigines are essentially distinguished from all other pagans on earth, in the uniform belief of most of them of one God; and their freedom from false gods; as well as in many other striking things, which appear in their history.[12]

Although the Native Americans do not comprise the entire company known as the Ten Lost Tribes of Israel, there is more than enough evidence to support the premise that they do have Israelite origins. And, since there is also evidence that their ancestors built the mounds, we have one more significant correlation between the Indians, the mounds, and the Book of Mormon, for the history contained in that holy text is of two great civilizations, one of which carried the blood of Israel in their veins.

~  ~  ~

To explore the early beginnings of the American Indians we must first travel back in time to the Nephite era described in the Book of Mormon. The Nephites, which had just recently arrived in the New World from Jerusalem, had divided into two factions early in their sojourn in the promised land, for the two elder sons of Lehi were rebellious and dissented from the family. Thus, they were ever after distinguished as "Lamanites," after the name of the eldest son, Laman. Moreover, because of their wicked natures, they were cursed with a dark skin and spent the remainder of their days warring with their more righteous brethren who were distinguished as "Nephites," after a younger son, Nephi. Unfortunately, even though the Nephites were a more righteous branch of the family, they, too, often turned to wickedness. This displeased the Lord greatly, for it was he who led them from harm's way and across the great waters to a new and fertile "promised land," where he had high hopes of raising up a righteous branch of Israel. Even so, as the centuries passed, and their wickedness became so gross he could no longer permit them to remain in the land, the Lord allowed their Lamanite brethren to utterly destroy them. So, yes, those who built the mounds were indeed from a "lost race," and yes, they can also be attributed to the Indians, for the remnants of that race, the victorious Lamanites (or Indians), continued to live on in the land throughout the ages.

Thus, those theories which pit one school of thought against the other can be easily reconciled with the inclusion of just one common denominator—the history contained in the Book of Mormon. That historical record, coupled with archeological findings, presents powerful evidence that the Native Americans did indeed spring from Israelitish stock. A branch which was led by the arm of the Lord from sure destruction in Jerusalem in 600 B.C. to a New World, a promised land, if you will, where they would flourish for nine hundred years.

~  ~  ~

Although wickedness over-took the Lamanites early in their sojourn in the land, their love of the Great Spirit and their devotion to him once enlightened, entitled them to blessings denied the Nephites because of their failure to remain steadfast in the faith of their fathers. We read in Enos of promises made to early prophets in regard to the Lamanites.

> And now behold, this was the desire which I desired of him—that if it should so be, that my people, the Nephites, should fall into transgression, and by any means be destroyed, and the Lamanites should not be destroyed, that the Lord God would preserve a record of my people, the Nephites; even if it so be by the power of his holy arm, that

it might be brought forth at some future day unto the Lamanites, that, perhaps, they might be brought unto salvation.

And the Lord responded:

Thy fathers have also required of me this thing; and it shall
be done unto them according to their faith; for their faith
was like unto thine. (Enos 1:13–18)

Although the Lamanites were steeped in wickedness,
they alone were permitted to remain in the promised land in
spite of the Lord's edict that only the righteous be allowed to
inhabit the land. Nonetheless, in compliance with that everlasting decree, they too, were eventually cleansed of their idolatrous behavior when Gentile Pilgrims began to flood the
promised land centuries later in preparation for the restitution
of all things.

~  ~  ~

Obviously, the Lamanites do not comprise the entire Ten
Lost Tribes of Israel, but we must not forget that both the
Nephites and Lamanites stemmed from Jacob, a direct descendant of Joseph—he who was sold into Egypt. Joseph was the
favorite son of Jacob the grand patriarch of that family. It was
Jacob who prophesied that Joseph's posterity would be as
"a fruitful bough, even a fruitful bough by a well, whose
branches run over the wall" (Gen. 49:22). Thus, in fulfillment
of prophecy, Joseph's posterity were led "over the wall" to a
promised land; a land choice above all; a land destined to be
their inheritance forever.

At some future point in time when the purposes of the
Lord are fulfilled, the Lord will once again bring the Lamanites to a clear understanding of their Creator. Once enlightened, he will gather them into the fold to sit side by side with
each of the other tribes of Israel, for they, too, are a portion of
that royal lineage and must not be forgotten. So yes, the Native
Americans did indeed carry with them Hebrew customs and

mannerisms, for their ancestors came directly from Jerusalem. This, of course, explains the obsession of those who believed they had Israelitish origins, for they did! Thus, it is easy to see why the public believed so firmly that the Mound Builders were the Ten Lost Tribes of Israel and remained unshaken in that belief for decades to come.

~  ~  ~

## Notes

1. Silverburg, *Mound Builders*, 41.
2. Ibid., 45.
3. Priest, *Wonders of Nature and Providence*, 312.
4. Ibid., 311–12.
5. Ibid., 314.
6. Ibid.,.316.
7. Ibid., 320.
8. Ibid.
9. Ibid., 321.
10. Ibid., 324.
11. Ibid., 230.
12. Ibid.

Nadaillac, *Pre-historic America*

## Chapter Three

# Relics of a Lost Nation

By the middle of the 1800s the woodlands were no longer sparsely populated. Small settlements were becoming towns and cities, and people who would have once given careless regard to the mounds on their properties were now planting and plowing with much more caution. Nonetheless, when mounds were discovered, all were quick to excavate them.

As exploration continued, curiosity about the mounds brought both amateurs and professionals alike into the field and more and more evidence of a vanished race began to emerge. It had long been known that the mounds entombed the dead, but no one expected to find quite so many. Thousands and thousands of bones were unearthed giving rise to speculation that the "valley of dry bones" seen by Ezekiel in vision (Ezekiel 37), were none other than the bones found scattered throughout the Ohio and Mississippi Valleys; surely they were those of Israel—just waiting in quiet repose for their day of redemption.

Bones of all ages were found, both young and old. Some were buried in carefully constructed tombs while others were thrown together promiscuously, as if hastily buried after a major disaster or war. But in both cases the dead were then covered with layers of earth, as if protecting against intrusion. In many instances, the mounds contained a succession of burials with one mound covered by another and still another until gigantic earthen monuments were erected. These strange mounds presented an awesome sight and, thus, the entire region seemed filled with mystery when colonists first entered the territory.

~ ~ ~

Not only did the mounds and their treasury of information indicate an ancient civilization once occupied the region, but Indian legends seemed to verify that same assumption—including one of a lost nation of giants. In 1819, John Heckewelder, a missionary who lived among the Indians for over forty years, recounts a legend told him by the Delaware, of their first migration to the more eastern regions of the country from the west. As their people neared the great Mississippi River, scouts were sent out to see what was on the other side. On their return they relayed the message, "that the country east of the Mississippi was inhabited by a very powerful nation who had many large towns." It was said they were remarkably tall and stout, and that there were giants among them. It was also said they built regular fortifications and entrenchments some of which Heckewelder himself had seen. One was on the Huron River, six or eight miles from Lake Erie; it consisted of two walls of earth with a deep ditch on one side and, nearby, "a number of large flat mounds." The legend had it that after numerous wars with their enemies, the original inhabitants ultimately fled down the Mississippi River and were never heard from again.[1]

Although Mr. Heckewelder's writings fueled a number of debates on the origin of the Indian tribes then occupying the territory, the legend that the ancient Mound Builders had been giants spawned another search: a search for the giant Mound Builders of the Ohio Valley. Robert Silverberg, in his *The Mound Builders*, comments:

> Few people wanted to believe that the Indians had built the mounds. The myth of the Mound Builders was a satisfying one; it was splendid to dream of a lost prehistoric race in the heart of America; if the vanished ones had been giants, or white men, or Israelites, or Toltecs, or Vikings, or Giant, white, Jewish, Toltec Vikings, so much the better.[2]

And so the search began, and not in vain, for giant skeletons were ultimately found, just as hoped. Harvey Rice describes a few excavated in 1800.

> Human bones of gigantic proportions were discovered in such a state of preservation as to be accurately described and measured. The cavities of the skulls were large enough in their dimensions to receive the entire head of a man of modern times, and could be put on one's head with as much ease as a hat or cap. The two jaw bones were sufficiently large to admit of being placed so as to match or fit the outside of a modern man's face. The other bones, so far as discovered, appeared to be of equal proportions with the skulls and jaw-bones, several of which have been preserved as relics in the cabinets of antiquarians, where they may still be seen.[3]

Not surprisingly, many large boned skeletons were found in the territory surrounding the Hill Cumorah (that area populated by those whose history is contained in the Book of Mormon.) O. Turner mentions a skeleton found at Aurora, New York, "which would indicate great height, exceeding by several inches, that of the tallest of our race." He comments further: "Some skeletons, almost entire have been exhumed, many of giant size, not less than seem to be eight feet in length."

In Cayuga County, New York, numerous giant skeletons were exhumed, which further established that the area had once been populated by people whose skulls and jawbones could cover the head and face of an ordinary man of our day. Moreover, legends of the area assert that a great destructive war was waged in the region, and "with such fury and determination on each side that practically all the warriors were slaughtered."[4]

Both Erie and Ontario Counties, New York, also yielded large numbers of giant skeletons. O. Turner mentioned that the "thigh bones" found in the region "would indicate great height exceeding by several inches the tallest of our race."[5]

In Fred Haughton's *Seneca Nation,* we read:

> In 1922, on the Rose farm, one half mile from Mormon Hill, a number of large skeletons, stone implements, copper ornaments, a copper axe of unusual type, and other articles were found. At this historical spot were found many of unusual physique, tall, long limbed, finely formed skulls, teeth finely shaped.[6]

Even local newspapers, such as Brown's *Western Gazetteer,* had much to say about the ancient burials in western New York, including the mention of skeletons "whose possessors were persons of gigantic stature."

Near Palmyra, New York, not far from the Hill Cumorah, a farmer unearthed several large skeletons while digging a cellar. He notified the Rochester Museum and scientists were quickly dispatched to help excavate the area. Six-foot skeletons were found which they estimated to be at least three thousand years old.

Numerous fortifications were also found in the area. Turner describes one such fort that "was within three miles of the Hill Cumorah which was "barricaded on an eminence, made for a large and powerful enemy. It must have been a very valuable place for defensive warfare." The entrenchment ten feet deep and twelve feet wide was plainly visible to the first settlers in that region." He commented further that skeletons found both within the enclosure and in the immediate vicinity clearly "indicate a race of men one-third larger than the present race."[7]

Silverburg mentioned that "bones of women over six feet in height and men approaching seven feet have been discovered." Thus, there is ample evidence that a nation of large and powerful people once lived in the region.

In their work, *Book of Mormon Geography,* McGavin and Bean noted, "that almost all the scientists and historians who discuss the subject use the same terms. It is surprising how many of them mention the giants who died on the ancient battlefields in the land of many waters, most of them insisting that the giant skeletons are to be found in the oldest ruins." Not surprisingly, these facts correspond beautifully with the scriptural accounts of both the Nephites and Jaredites, who were said to have had many large and mighty men among them—undoubtedly the ancestors of these tribes of giants.

> And it came to pass that I, Nephi, being exceedingly young, nevertheless being large in stature. (1 Ne. 2:16)

> And it came to pass that in the first year of the reign of Alma in the judgment—seat, there was a man brought before him to be judged, a man who was large, and noted for his much strength. (Alma 1:2)

> And they were led by a man whose name was Coriantumr; and he was a descendant of Zarahemla; and he was a dissenter from among the Nephites; and he was a large and a mighty man. (Hel. 1:15)

> And the brother of Jared being a large and mighty man. (Ether 1:34)

> And it came to pass that they ate and slept, and prepared for death on the morrow. And they were large and mighty men as to the strength of men. (Ether 15:26)

Thus, the picture emerges of a large and mighty nation living in the near vicinity of the Hill Cumorah and throughout the entire mound building region—the giant, Mound Builders

Grave Creek Mound.
Squier and Davis, *Ancient Monuments*, 1848.

so long sought for; a people who bear remarkable similarities to those described in the Book of Mormon.

Much of what we have learned of that ancient people have come to us from the various antiquities found in their burial sites. One of the most impressive excavated was the Grave Creek Mound in Virginia in 1838. Mr. Atwater, who

Shaft in Grave Creek Mound. Squier and Davis, *Ancient Monuments*, 1848.

wrote a paper on the mound, said it was: "one of the most august monuments of remote antiquity anywhere to be found; its circumference at the base was 300 yards, its diameter, of course 100. Its altitude from measurement is 90 ft. and its diameter, at the summit is 45 ft." The owner of the property excavated just far enough to discover it contained thousands of skeletons and, then, in deference to the dead, refused to allow further work. In 1838, however, another member of the family, Abelard B. Tomlinson, started limited excavation. Rather than desecrate the entire burial site, he simply sank a shaft from the top of the mound to its base and ultimately discovered skeletons and artifacts at various levels. The relics that were found within proved invaluable to the world of archaeology.

~  ~  ~

As time passed, it soon became apparent that even their mode of burial was significant, for burial techniques give vital clues to the antiquity of such interments, as well as to the cultural differences between distinct and separate groups of people. One thing seemed certain to all, however. The skeletons interred within the mounds were of a very great age. We learn in David Baldwin's *Ancient America*:

> Great antiquity is indicated by the skeleton taken from the mounds. Every skeleton of a Mound-Builder is found in a condition of extreme decay. It sometimes appears that the surface of a mound has been used by the wild Indians for interments; but their skeletons, which are always found well preserved, can be readily distinguished by their position in the mounds, as well as by other peculiarities. The decayed bones of Mound-Builders are invariable found within the mounds, never on the surface, usually at the bottom of the structure, and nearly always "in such a state of decay as to render all attempts to restore the skull, or, indeed, any part of the skeleton, entirely hopeless. . ." Not more than one or two skeletons of that people have been recovered in a condition suitable for intelligent examination. . . . All the circumstances attending their burial were unusually favorable for their preservation. The earth around them has invariably been found "wonderfully compact and dry." And yet, when exhumed, they are in such a decomposed and crumbling condition that to restore them is impossible. Sound and well-preserved skeletons, known to be nearly two thousand years old, have been taken from burial-places in England, and other European countries less favorable for preserving them. The condition of an ancient skeleton can not be used as an accurate measure of time, but it is sufficiently accurate to show the difference between the ancient and the modern, and in this case it allows us to assume that these extremely decayed skeletons of the Mound-Builders are much more than two thousand years old."[8]

Archeologists tell us that artifacts found in various mounds help identify different cultures and time periods. They believe those from more archaic periods were utilitarian while those from later periods were more ornamental. Thus, artifacts such as shell beads, pearls, rings, bracelets, breastplates, and even metal crowns all provide important information as to the cultural habits of each region. The "Turner Mounds in Hamilton County, Ohio," for example, "contained 12,000 unperforated pearls, 35,000 pearl beads, 20,000 shell beads, and nuggets of copper, meteoric iron and silver as well as small sheets of hammered gold, copper, iron beads, and more,"[9] which showed evidence of a superior culture.

Treasures of invaluable historical information were found in several mounds. One such mound was described as follows:

> A tall young man and a young woman lay side by side. 'At the head, neck hips, and knees of the female and completely encircling the skeleton were thousands of pearl beads and buttons of wood and stone covered in copper; extending the full length of the grave along one side was a row of copper ear ornaments; at the wrists of the female were copper bracelets; copper ear ornaments adorned the ears of both, and both wore necklaces of grizzly-bear canines and copper breastplates on the chest.'[10]

Antler headdresses in the Cresap Mound indicate the impersonation of animals may have been an important part of the Mississippian Culture, while long tube shaped artifacts give rise to speculation that they knew the art of astronomy.

Bird pipe. Squier and Davis, *Ancient Monuments*, 1848.

The size and shape of smoking pipes were also studied, for literally thousands were found throughout the mound building region. Thus, both the mode of burial as well as the artifacts found in their burial sites were important in formulating ideas about the culture of these ancient people and at what point in history they lived.

Many beautiful artifacts were unearthed, including statues and vases with intricate detail. Pottery and trinkets such as rings and bracelets were found by the thousands, as were arrowheads and various weapons of war. Not surprisingly, the more artifacts

Beaver pipe. Squier and Davis, *Ancient Monuments,* 1848.

unearthed in the area, the more convinced the people were that they were created by a a superior culture.

Baldwin believed the pottery found rivaled those found in Peru. Although others felt he had exaggerated somewhat, we would only have to look at the vases unearthed in Ohio to agree with that assessment.

It appears the Mound Builders also had the art of spinning and weaving, for cloth has also been found among their remains. Other grave goods include, "Gulf Coast conch shell beakers, jewelry made of Lake Superior copper and mete-

Pottery from the mounds. Squier and Davis, *Ancient Monuments,* 1848.

orite iron. There are beautiful bannerstones and birdstones, mica cutouts, highly polished, incised sandstone and limestone tablets, zoomorphic platforms and tubular pipes, pottery urns and figures."[11]

Statues were also unearthed which showed the strength of their artistic achievements. Those who viewed these remarkable relics refused to believe that the "savages" of their day had wrought them. Moreover, they considered them so dissimilar to the works of the more historic Indians that the "vanished race" theory continued to grow in popularity.

In spite of the continuing debates on the subject of the mounds, the great age of the various artifacts inferred within them made it obvious to all that a superior race once thrived in the region in times of great antiquity. David Baldwin comments:

> When we consider the time required to people the whole extent of the territory where their remains are found, and bring that people into a condition to construct such monuments, and when we reflect on the interval that must have passed after their construction until the epoch of their abandonment, we are constrained to accord them a very high antiquity.[12]

Other incredible works were also found, and today they line the halls of numerous museums throughout the northeast. It would be difficult to dismiss the artistic achievements of these noble races after gazing for a moment at their treasures.

~ ~ ~

Blackware jar representing an animal. Courtesy Museum of the American Indian, Smithsonian Institution, 17/3260.

As the mounds gave up their dead, more and more information was gleaned about the ancient inhabitants of the region. Every evidence indicates they were an industrious people who made implements of both war and husbandry and delighted in the manufacture of ornaments for both male and female, young and old. They spun cloth and made pottery, some rather simple and others more exotic, which they often traded with other parts of the mound building regions. Not surprisingly, the scriptures tell us essentially the same about the Nephites and the Jaredites, for both worked all kinds of ores, built impressive buildings, and were an intelligent and beautiful people.

> And we multiplied exceedingly, and spread upon the face of the land, and became exceedingly rich in gold, and in silver, and in precious things, and in fine workmanship of wood, in buildings, and in machinery. (Jarom 1:8)

Michigan Relic, depicting building
with strange inscriptions over entrance.
Courtesy Museum of Church History and Art,
The Church of Jesus Christ of Latter-day Saints.

The scriptures clearly indicate that buildings were erected, yet because they were constructed of wood, remnants of such structures have not survived the ages. However, tablets unearthed in Michigan, and dating to the Christian era, depict grand edifices, some of which stood three stories high, often with strange inscriptions over the entrances. If authentic, they would give clear indication that a civilization much like the Nephites lived in the region; a people who erected buildings, just as described in the scriptures.

Such relics, along with various other pertinent discoveries, indicate that two different cultures lived during the Mound Building Epoch, with one apparently living an entirely different lifestyle than the other. While certain artifacts reveal that one culture lived in more highly organized societies, the other appears to have had a caste system, with the elite occupying the most commanding grounds within the mound centers and the general populace living in tents within the compound or in nearby farming communities. This is also consistent with the scriptures, for they inform us the Lamanites lived a culturally different lifestyle than the Nephites. Moreover, they while they reveal that many of the Lamanites occupied cities in Book of Mormon territory, they also inform us that many lived in tents much as many of the Mound Builders did.

> Now, the more idle part of the Lamanites lived in the wilderness, and dwelt in tents; and they were spread through the wilderness on the west, in the land of Nephi; yea, and also on the west of the land of Zarahemla, in the borders by the seashore, and on the west in the land of Nephi, in the place of their fathers' first inheritance, and thus bordering along by the seashore. (Alma 22:28)

Without the scriptures to rely on for information relative to the ancient inhabitants of the area and their lifestyles, the mystery surrounding the mounds and those who built them continued to plague the populace during the eighteenth and nineteenth centuries. Those who found evidence to support the premise that a race similar to our modern-day Indians occupied the region during the mound building epoch, tried in every conceivable way to prove their point. Not surprisingly, those who believed that a superior culture once lived in the region spent just as much time trying to prove their position. It was simply inconceivable to either side that both were correct. Thus, the debates continued for generations.

~  ~  ~

## Notes

1. Silverberg, *Mound Builders,* 46–47.
2. Ibid., 48.
3. McGavin and Bean, *Geography of the Book of Mormon,* 11–12.
4. Ibid., 13.
5. Ibid., 13.
6. Ibid., 13.
7. Ibid., 14.

8. Baldwin, *Ancient America,* 48–49.
9. Silverburg, *Mound Builders,* 218.
10. Ibid., 218.
11. Korp, *Sacred Geography,* 17.
12. Baldwin, *Ancient America,* 53.

Chapter Four

# The Art of Metallurgy

The commonly held belief that an enlightened people once occupied the woodlands was due, in part, to the fact that articles of metal had been discovered in the mounds. This fact alone convinced many a skeptic that a nation far more enlightened than the Indians once lived in the region. The discovery of lumps of lead ore, a sheet of copper, and stones with hieroglyphics on them in a mound in Ohio helped solidify that notion.

In subsequent excavations of the same mound, even more artifacts were found, including human skeletons, a number of beads, shells, and some copper objects in the form of curved plates connected by hollow rods. These impressive finds reinforced the growing body of evidence that the art of working in metal had been known by the early inhabitants of the area and were often mentioned as proof of their superiority. In fact, as time passed, more and more evidence seemed to support that idea. Thus, the prevailing notion that a superior race once occupied the territory gained in popularity, and a new wave of interest in mound exploration began.

More spectacular evidence surfaced in 1819, while excavating in a mound in Marietta, Ohio. Samuel Hildreth, a local doctor, found objects made of silver and copper and some broken pieces of copper tube filled with iron rust. Hildreth guessed they were from the lower end of a scabbard, however, no sword was found. This find raised the temperature even further on the theory that the mounds were built by a nation familiar with the art of metallurgy, for "it appeared the copper and silver had been joined by the difficult process of plating." For a time this notion was accepted. But, as more and more time passed, scholars made every effort to discount it, for it placed their own theories in jeopardy—namely, that the region had not been visited by outsiders prior to Columbus.

Because of the growing number of mounds being destroyed, Caleb Atwater, a noted archeologist, began his own search for evidence supporting his theory that the Mound Builders were superior to the ordinary Indians of his day. His efforts in that pursuit eventually paid off when he succeeded in finding an artifact that resembled a plate of cast iron. He knew that, if authenticated, it would lend further credence to the theory that a noble race of people once populated the woodlands. His description of the find goes as follows:

> The handle, either of a small sword, or a large knife, made of an elk's horn; around the end where a blade had been inserted, was a ferule of silver, which, though black, was not much injured by time; though the handle showed the hole where the blade had been inserted, yet no iron was found, but an oxide or rust remained, of similar shape and size. . . . About twenty feet to the north of it (i.e. a skeleton previously mentioned in his report) was another, with which was found a large mirror. . . . On this mirror was a plate of iron, which had become an oxide, but before it was disturbed by the spade, resembled a plate of cast iron.[1]

Now, because of the on-going war of ideas regarding the treasures found within the mounds, and in spite of this first hand description of the account, it was concluded by the scholars of his day that "the metal found in the Circleville mound was probably 'raw meteoric iron,' not 'cast iron' at all." Such curt dismissals of such a significant find were prevalent among various theorists of this era. However as time passed, an agent from the Smithsonian found a similar piece of antler in a North Carolina mound "in which still remained a part of the iron implement of which it formed the handle." Moreover, " chemical analysis showed that this was *not* meteoric iron."[2] Thus, the former artifact could no longer be dismissed quite so easily.

In the *12th Annual Report of the Bureau of Ethnology* we read comments on Atwater's earlier discovery:

> Mr. Atwater says he was present when the mound was removed and "carefully examined the contents." . . . As the minuteness of detail as to size and relative position, of articles in the mound indicate that he took notes at the time, his statements of fact as to what he saw should not be rejected because they do not agree with a preconceived theory— especially as he was the best qualified and most careful observer of his day in this line.[3]

Those who believed the mounds had been built by the ancestors of the modern Indians and not some mysterious "lost race" would have none of it, however, and looked for another explanation—one that would discourage such a view and would draw people back to their own way of thinking. Thus, in spite of the fact that iron artifacts had been found in the mound, a few relics of obvious European origins were discovered as well, which gave the opposing theorists the out they were looking for. They simply solved the problem by relegating a good many of the metal relics found to a European origin.

Mr. Conant, A.M. member of the St. Louis Academy of Science, and of the American Association for the Advancement of Science, comments further on that subject:

> There are certain facts which have been quoted from time to time, which fit into none of the popular theories concerning the state of the arts of the Mound-builders. It

has been stated, and often repeated, that they had no knowledge of smelting or casting metals, yet the recent discoveries in Wisconsin of implements of copper cast in molds—as
well as the molds themselves, of various patterns, and
wrought with much skill—prove that the age of metallurgi-
cal arts had dawned in that region at least.

And again: what shall be said concerning the traces of
iron implements which have been discovered from time
to time in the mounds, but more frequently at great depths
below the surface of the soil. Though accounts of such discoveries are generally from reliable sources, they have lat-
terly received no attention, and always have been considered
as so much perilous ware which no one cared to handle.[4]

He comments further:

And to question whether they possessed a knowledge
of working iron, the wise man will hesitate long before he
answers in the negative. It should be remembered, too, how
quickly—unless under the most favoring conditions—iron
corrodes to dust and leaves scarcely a trace behind.[5]

Although controversies over whether or not the Mound
Builders knew the art of metallurgy continued for quite some
time, it was obvious that copper was their metal of choice, for
literally thousands of copper relics had been found throughout
the region. The most prevalent were ornamental in nature such
as arm bands and rings, which were placed on even the infants
before their burials.

Josiah Priest, a noted antiquarian, comments on the various metal artifacts found in the mounds:

A vast many instances of articles made of copper and
sometimes plated with silver, have been met with on open-
ing their works. Circular pieces of copper, intended either
as medals or breastplates, have been found, several inches
in diameter, very much injured by times. In several tumuli
the remains of knives and even of swords, in the form of
rust, have been discovered. . . . But besides, there have been
found very well manufactured swords and knives of iron,

and possibly steel, says Mr. Atwater; from which we are to conclude the primitive people of America, either discovered the use of iron themselves, as the Greeks did, . . . or that they carried a knowledge of this ore with them at the time of their dispersion.[6]

Nothing could be closer to the truth than this last statement, for the scriptures inform us that at the time of their dispersion the Jaredites brought the art of metallurgy with them to the New World.

The Book of Mormon informs us that they

did buy and sell and traffic one with another, that they might get gain.

And they did work in all manner of ore, and they did make gold and silver, and iron, and brass and all manner of metals; and they did dig it out of the earth; wherefore, they did cast up mighty heaps of earth to get ore, of gold, and of silver, and of iron, and of copper. And they did work all manner of fine work. . . .

And they did make all manner of tools to till the earth, both to plow and to sow, to reap and to hoe, and also to thrash.

And they did make all manner of tools with which they did work their beasts.

And they did make all manner of weapons of war. And they did work all manner of work of exceedingly curious workmanship. (Ether 10:22–23, 25–27)

We are informed in Ether 7:9 that king Shule "did molten out of the hill, and made swords of steel." The fact that he *did molten* out of the hill Ephraim the ore used to produce the steel clearly indicates the art of metallurgy was well known among the Jaredites, who lived in the region from a time shortly after the Great Flood to about 600 B.C.

Not only do the scriptures inform us that the art of working in metals was well known among the Ancients, but archeological evidence also supports that premise. Ash carbon tests

Copper breastplate, Wayne May, *Ancient American Magazine.*

conducted by the University of Michigan demonstrate the copper mines in the upper Great Lakes region were worked as far back as 3000 B.C., "by unknown miners of great skill and incredible labor, excavating an minimum estimated 500,000 tons of copper."[7] While some suggest even earlier dates, Professor James P. Sherz, of the University of Wisconsin, informs us that "Radio-carbon tests indicate the mines were worked most heavily between 3,000–1,000 B.C.,"[8] a time which extended well into the Jaredite era. Although little remains of that ancient civilization, archeologists have come to believe the archaic populations of the region were definitely advanced enough to have worked the various mines in Wisconsin, Upper Michigan, and Ontario, Canada. Five thousand mines have been found on Michigan's Keewenaw Peninsula alone, and nearly as many on Isle Royale, which "had easily accessible veins that yielded nuggets of almost pure copper." In fact, so much copper was taken from the mines during that ancient era that many still wonder where it all went.

> Here on Isle Royale and on the Upper Michigan Peninsula, 500,000 tons of pure copper (one billion pounds) had been mined out according to estimates of metallurgical engineers. This incredible amount of copper has not been accounted for by American archeologists—the sum total according to archeological findings here in the states amounts to a mere handful of copper beads and trinkets—float copper. Five hundred thousand tons of pure copper does not disintegrate into thin air—it cannot be sneezed away—it must be somewhere and, to date, it has not been located in the United States.[9]

Mining operations of this size would be tremendous. One report states, "it would have taken 10,000 men 1,000 years, with crude stone mauls as their only tool, to have accomplished the vast operation." Professor Octave J. DuTemple comments:

> There was certainly some great economic demand to support such operations with men, material, food and transpiration. The massive effort could not have been put forth to secure copper for mere trinkets and ornaments, but rather working tools, probably for armaments, and to exchange in trade.[10]

While Lake Superior copper has been traced to Central America and prehistoric Mexico, some speculate that much of it was transported as far away as Egypt where large numbers of copper tools were used to build their "statues, temples, and tombs." Others suggest it was transported to the Mediterranean where huge amounts of copper were used for their armaments and tools. Some even speculate that much was transported to the mysterious Island "Atlantis," which supposedly disappeared into the Ocean along with all its inhabitants following some terrible catastrophe. But, interestingly, although such massive amounts of copper do not show up in the United States, "they do not show up in third and fourth Millennium Europe either."

Speculation over where such massive amounts of copper may have been taken fill numerous books and articles. Even the routes used to transport the copper out of the region have been suggested:

> Copper from the mines was transported across Lake Superior, through Lake Huron, across the French River in Ontario, then down the Ottawa River to the waiting ancient Europeans at Montreal. This is the same route used by French-Canadians for the beaver trade from the 17th to 19th Centuries.[11]

Others suggest they followed the Trent-Severn River system, which flows through the center of the South Ontario isthmus/peninsula from central Lake Huron down to Lake Ontario.

In his article "Who Mined Great Lakes' Copper 4,000 Years Ago?" Jim Grimes comments:

> World temperatures were 4 to 6 degrees warmer than today, thereby allowing agriculture and animal husbandry to thrive in regions of both Scandinavia and North America. Then, as now, voyagers could cross the North Atlantic Ocean by hopping Ireland—Faeroes—Iceland—Greenland—Labrador without being out of sight of land for more than six days at a time during an entire voyage.[12]

Thus, not only did the copper mines of the upper Great Lakes bless those upon this continent, but many suggest it may have blessed other countries as well.

~ ~ ~

The fact that great amounts of copper was mined at such a remote time in history should not be surprising to those familiar with the Book of Mormon, however, for the Lord informed the brother of Jared that their seed would be greatly blessed,

> and there shall be none greater than the nation which I will raise up unto me of thy seed, upon all the face of the earth. (Ether 1:43)

The production of copper would certainly have aided in their prosperity, especially in such massive amounts. But, around 1200–1000 B.C., and for reasons still unknown, the mining operations in the upper Great Lakes came to an abrupt halt. Many suggest this time coincides with the end of the European Bronze Age, when techniques for processing iron were developed and the demand for copper dropped off considerably. Kenneth Caroli explains:

> The Michigan mines began concurrent with the Near Eastern Bronze Age, expanding coeval with its major phases, circa 2000 B.C. (Middle Bronze Age), 1500 B.C. (Start of the late Bronze Age), and 1300 B.C. (Final phase of the Lake Bronze Age). About 1200 B.C. the mines were abandoned with startling suddenness at the very moment

the Old World of the Late Bronze Age fell into chaos, its trade networks collapsing. All this seems too much of a coincidence to be one.[13]

Even so, the world of archeology has been at a loss to explain the sudden and complete end to such extensive mining operations. Those who came across these dormant mines said it appeared that those who worked the mines laid down their tools with every intention of picking them up the very next day. Yet, there is no evidence that they were worked from that time forth. Now, even though the markets for copper appear to have been drying up at his period in history, that does not seem to adequately explain the sudden and complete halt to all mining operations. Thus, a different scenario altogether might be suggested.

Fancy copper workings. Photo, Wayne May, *Ancient American Magazine.*

While, modern dating methods can indicate the time various mines in the upper Great Lakes were in operation, it would be difficult, at best, to be certain of just when all mining operations actually ended. Although as some speculate, the great amounts of copper mined during the Bronze Age may have stopped earlier, it would seem reasonable to suggest that lessor amounts were excavated throughout the entire Jaredite era. Thus, we might reasonably suggest that the sudden cessation to all mining operations was due to the terrible internal conflict that ultimately precipitated the fall of that mighty empire around 600 B.C This was a terrible time; a time when opposing factions led the people into one of the greatest wars of all time.

So great and lasting had been the war, and so long had been the scene of bloodshed and carnage that the whole face of the land was covered with the bodies of the dead.

And so swift and speedy was the war that there was none left to bury the dead, but they did march forth from the shedding of blood to the shedding of blood, leaving the bodies of both men, women, and children strewed upon the face of the land, to become a prey to the worms of the flesh. (Ether 14:22–23)

Millions were slain, yet still the war continued. Then, in a final effort for victory, a time of gathering took place. Every man, woman, and child still living was ultimately gathered to the land of many waters in what is now New York state. Thus, understandably, every phase of industry would have halted at this point in history -including their mining operations.

At the end of four years of gathering, the last remnants of that mighty nation were poised for attack around the Hill Ramah for one of the greatest battles of all time; one so all-encompassing it caused the extinction of their entire civilization. Only one lone soul survived that terrible blood-bath. The entire nation had become so corrupt and so steeped in wickedness over the course of their millennium and a half stay in the promised land, that the Lord withdrew his Spirit and allowed them to destroy one another. Unfortunately, we must wait until the ancient records are restored to learn the total and complete story of that terribly time in history. For now, all we can do is speculate.

~  ~  ~

The scriptures inform us that the Nephites, who entered the land shortly after the demise of the Jaredite Nation, also had a knowledge of metallurgy. Although there is ample evidence that they, too, worked in copper, archeological evidence indicates they did not mine it as extensively as the former occupants had.

> And we multiplied exceedingly, and spread upon the
> face of the land, and became exceedingly rich in gold, and
> in silver, and in precious things, and in fine workmanship of
> wood, in buildings, and in machinery, and also in iron and
> copper, and brass and steel, making all manner of tools of
> every kind to till the ground, and weapons of war—yea, the
> sharp pointed arrow, and the quiver, and the dart, and the
> javelin, and all preparations for war. (Jarom 1:8)

Such scriptures make it abundantly clear that the refining of all kinds of metals was common during ancient times—including that of brass. Once again, archeological evidence bears this out as well, for numerous artifacts of both copper and brass have been found throughout the mound building region—especially in western New York, the very region so much warfare took place during both the Nephite and Jaredite eras. The following account of such discoveries is most interesting.

> In Scipio, (about 45 miles from Cumorah) on Salmon
> Creek, a Mr. Halsted has, from time to time during ten years
> past, ploughed up, from a certain. extent of land of his farm,
> seven or eight hundred pounds of brass, which appeared to
> have once been formed into various implements, both of
> husbandry and war; helmets and working utensils mingled
> together. The finder of this brass, we are informed as he dis-
> covered it carried it to Auburn, and sold it by the pound,
> where it was worked up, with as little curiosity attending as
> though it had been but an ordinary article of the country's
> produce.[14]

The historian Smith comments on the industry of those who worked the various copper mines found throughout the region:

> Who can imagine the Iroquois or Algonquins working
> the copper mines with such intelligence and skill, and such
> a combination of systematic and persistent industry! They
> had no traditions of such a condition of life, no trace of it.
> It is absurd to suppose a relationship, or a connection of any
> kind, between the original barbarism of the Indians and the

civilization of the Mound-builders. The two people were entirely distinct and separate from each other. If they really belonged to the same race, which is extremely doubtful, we must go back through unnumbered ages to find their common origin and the date of their separation.[15]

It is interesting to note just how close so many come to the truth without actually finding it. Nonetheless, the fact the Ancients worked in metal is becoming more and more accepted with the passing of time, especially in light of the fact that iron and steel implements are being discovered all over the country.

Seldom do we hear of gold, however, yet the Book of Mormon constantly mentions the use of gold. Now, it is entirely possible that the gold reserves available to both the Nephites and Jaredites were eventually all used up, much as they were in California during the gold rush of the 1800s. But the few references to gold in the region is enough to indicate this precious metal was available to both the Nephites and Jaredites.

In E. G. Squier's book, *Ancient Monuments of the Mississippi Valley,* we read:

> It is asserted by the Portuguese chronicler of De Sotos' ill-fated expedition, that copper hatchets were found in possession of some of the Indian tribes along the Gulf, 'which were said to have a mixture of gold.' These, the Spaniards were told, were obtained in a province towards the north, called Chisca, "where there was a melting of copper, and of another metal of the same color, save that it was finer and far better to the sight, which they used not so much, because it was softer.' The Spaniards did not visit the province of Chisca; as they were informed high mountains intervened, which could not be passed with horses.[16]

When the French first arrived off the coast of Florida, they said that both gold and silver was obtained from the Indians in rich abundance. In their own colorful vernacular we read:

> It seemeth they had estimation of their gold and silver, for it is wrought flat and graven, which they wear about

their necks, some others round like a pancake with a hole in the midst to bolster up their breasts withal.[17]

In 1825, fifty miles north of Atlanta, near where the town of Dahlonega stands, a gold mine was discovered that had the appearance of being worked at some remote period in time. Unfortunately, the Indians knew nothing of it. This mine produced so much gold it sparked a gold rush and people from far and near came on foot and horseback in hopes of gaining instant wealth.[14] Hopefully, other such mines will one day surface, adding further credence to the Book of Mormon's reference to gold.

~　~　~

Because of the mounting evidence that the ancient Mound Builders worked in metals, which suggested a superior race once inhabited the region, speculations about their origins continued to surface. Books were written by the dozens—some even becoming best sellers. Their stories were of lost empires who were

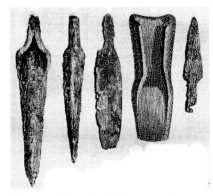

Copper articles. 1. 12-in. spear; 2. spear; 3. knife blade; 4. chisel; 5. knife. Squier and Davis, *Ancient Monuments,* 1848.

"dragged down to destruction by hordes of barbarians." Yet, in spite of all the artifacts found, and all the theories being presented, no one seemed to agree on the origin of the lost civilization belonging to the Mound Builders. Numerous theories arose over the years, but two major schools of thought prevailed. One, insisting that the Mound Builders were an ancient civilization, far surpassing the present-day Indians in skill and intelligence; a civilization enlightened enough to have built cities and create beautiful artifacts, and artistic enough to have produced fine pottery, beautiful statues, and even curious metal works. The other theory insisting the mounds were simply the product of the ancestors of the modern Indians who continued to build and inhabit them until the time of European contact. It was still inconceivable to them that both theories were correct.

~ ~ ~

## Notes

1. Priest, *American Antiquities,* 185.
2. Thomas, *12th Annual Report of the Bureau of Ethnology,* 716.
3. Ibid., 717.
4. Conant, *Foot-prints of Vanished Races,* 108–9.
5. Ibid., 109–10.
6. Priest, *American Antiquities,* 265.
7. Caroli, *Ancient American Magazine,*13.
8. Scherz, *Ancient American Magazine,* 3.
9. Mertz, *Atlantis,* 65.
10. DuTemple, "Prehistory's Greatest Mystery," 10.
11. Grimes, "Who Mined Great Lakes' Copper," 29.
12. Ibid.
13. Caroli, *Ancient American Magazine,* 14.
14. Priest, *American Antiquities,* 259–62.
15. McGavin and Bean, *Geography of the Book of Mormon,* 82.
16. Squier and Davis, *Ancient Monuments of the Mississippi Valley,* 199.
17. Thomas, *12th Annual Report of the Bureau of Ethnology,* 712.

Engraved Michigan
Relic. Courtesy
Wayne May.

Inscribed tablet,
Michigan Relic.
Courtesy Wayne May.

Chapter Five

# Ancient Tablets

While the world of archeology argued over the authenticity of various metal artifacts, numerous tablets with strange inscriptions on them were being unearthed all over the mound building region. Needless to say this sparked renewed interest in the Lost Race theory, for if they proved to be genuine, it would greatly increase the believability that a superior culture once populated the woodlands. Yet, true to form, as each tablet was discovered, various authorities were ready and waiting to question its authenticity.

Even so, one particular discovery made in 1860 gained instant notoriety, for it appeared to have genuine Israelitish origins. A stone was found with the pictograph of a bearded man in a long flowing robe along with a Hebrew abridgment of the Ten Commandments. Even more impressive was the fact that the Hebrew name for Moses was etched on its surface. Yet because it was found in Newark, Ohio, the seat of known forgery experts, the stone was under immediate suspicion. Then, when the man who discovered it died and an old

Hebrew Bible was found by his bedside, the stone was condemned as a fake without further discussion—supposing the Bible had been used to help create the controversial artifact. Others, on the other hand, were equally convinced he used the Bible to decipher the inscriptions and not for the purpose of fraud. Thus, the controversy over its authenticity continues still.

Now, we learn in Mormon 9:32–34 that the Hebrew language had been altered by the Nephites. Therefore, we have reason to be cautious about making any hasty judgment in favor of their authenticity. Yet, neither can we entirely discount the possibility that at least some of their religious instructions may have been written in the pure archaic form. Thus, they cannot be summarily dismissed as fraudulent either. We must also take into account the fact that others the Lord might have led to the promised land over the years, may have also written in Hebrew. Therefore, we must be cautious of any quick determination.

The comments of B. H. Roberts, editor of *The History of the Church,* regarding various inscribed tablets found throughout the region are most interesting:

> For my own part . . . I see no reason to doubt the existence of these relics in America before the advent of the Spaniards. According to the Book of Mormon the ancient inhabitants of America, the Nephites, had the writings of Moses. The Ten Commandments were regarded as the summing up, the crystallization of the law of God to the people pending the advent of Messiah with the more perfect law of the gospel. What could be more natural than that they should multiply copies of these scriptures . . . That the Nephites did multiply copies of the scriptures that they had in their possession (and doubtless also copies of striking passages of those scriptures) is evident from what is said upon the subject by Mormon when giving an account of the transfer of the Nephite records from one Shiblon to Helaman, the son of Helaman; "Now, behold, all those engravings which were in the possession of Helaman, were written and sent forth among the children of men throughout all the land, save it were those parts which had been commanded

by Alma should not go forth." . . . There was perfect liberty
to multiply copies of the scriptures, and that it was done is
further evidenced from the fact that missionaries from the
Nephites to the Lamanites are found to be in possession of
copies of the scriptures which Lehi's colony brought with
them from Jerusalem and from which they read for the
instruction of their hearer. (See Alma 37.) It is not difficult
to believe, in light of these facts, that noted personages
among native Americans should have engraven on stone . . .
passages of the holy scripture; nor is it incredible that these
should be buried with them—since to bury one's personal
effects with him was a custom of the natives. . . . The fact of
the discovery is beyond question; the nature of them is strong
incidental proof of the claims of the Book of Mormon.[1]

The Nephites were constantly being admonished to read
the scriptures, which clearly indicates that such tablets were
not uncommon.

> Now behold, my brethren, I would ask if ye have read
> the scriptures? If ye have, how can ye disbelieve on the Son
> of God? (Alma 33:14)

Other discoveries give added support to the premise that
ancient Americans inscribed on tablets—including metal tablets.

> Mr. Benjamin E. Styles of Cincinnati, Ohio, while
> excavating the earth for a cistern, in the year 1847, found a
> few feet above high water mark on the Ohio river, a gold
> plate. It was thrown out with the loose earth while excavat-
> ing about nine feet beneath the surface. Said plate is of fine
> gold, three or four inches in length, averaging about three-
> fourths of an inch in width, about one-eight of an inch in
> thickness, with the edges scalloped. In the face of which
> was beautifully set another plate of the same material, and
> fastened together by two pins, running through both. This
> latter plate is full of ancient raised characters, beautifully
> engraved upon its surface; the whole exhibiting fine work-
> manship. The plate was examined by Dr. Wise, in a very
> learned Rabbi of the Jewish synagogue in Cincinnati, and
> editor of a Hebrew paper there, who pronounced the char-
> acters to be mostly ancient Egyptian.[2]

(The fact the characters were mostly Egyptian is of no small importance here, for the scriptures inform us the Nephites wrote in reformed Egyptian.)

~ ~ ~

The prevailing notion that the mounds were the work of a lost race of civilized people continued to intrigued a large portion of the population during the eighteenth and nineteenth centuries, and they longed for some proof to substantiate such claims. They had high hopes that, at least, some of these inscribed tablets would help in that pursuit. But, as might be expected, critics were always ready with a quick response designed to discredited any and all inscribed relics, as well as those who found them.

Unfortunately, a number of forgery rings did exist in those days, made up of unscrupulous men who wished to cash in on the growing demand for ancient relics. To make matters worse, some tablets were labeled fakes for no other reason than to cast aspersions on their finders. Such measures were all too often used to cloud the issues further in their own vain attempts to come out the victors in the continuing debates on the origins of the Mound Builders. The whole matter was so mired in deception and mystery that eventually all inscribed tablets were looked upon with suspicion and given little chance for study. Thus, Lucifer's design to discredit any and all evidences of those whose history is contained in the Book of Mormon was finding a measure of success. However, far too many tablets were discovered to dismiss them all.

We learn in Adair's *History of the American Indians* that even the Indians had metal tablets which they claim came from the person the white men called God.

> In the Tuccabatches on the Tallapoose river, thirty miles above the Allabahamah garrison are two brazen tables, and five of copper. They (the Indians) esteem them so sacred as to keep them constantly in their holy of holies, without

touching them in the least, only in the time of their com-pounded first-fruit offering, and annual expiation of sins.[3]

Still another interesting tablet was discovered in the Grave Creek Mound in 1838. "It was an oval white sandstone disc, 3/4 of an inch thick and 1 1/2 inches in diameter, on which was inscribed three lines of an unknown alphabet."[4] Unfortunately, because the inscriptions resembled the alphabet of so many different languages, including what some believed were Greek, Phoenician, Hebrew, Celtic, Libyan, and Canaanite, no one could translate it. Therefore, it was simply set aside as a fraud; and so it was with many tablets.

The fact that no one could translate such strange inscriptions should not be surprising to those familiar with the Book of Mormon, however, for the Lord revealed to the brother of Jared that no one would be able to read their records without the aid of the Seer Stones. Thus, the fact that the tablets were inscribed in a language unknown to the world of academia, may actually prove their authenticity and also provides an additional link between the Mound Builders and the people of the Book of Mormon.

> And behold, . . . ye shall write them in a language that they cannot be read.
>
> And behold, these two stones will I give unto thee, and ye shall seal them up also with the things which ye shall write,
>
> For behold, the language which ye shall write I have confounded; wherefore I will cause in my own due time that these stones shall magnify to the eyes of men these things which ye shall write. (Ether 3:22–24)

As time passed, still other tablets surfaced, many of which were inscribed with the same strange mixture of cuneiform, Egyptian hieroglyph, Phoenician and Greek letters. Once again, because the inscriptions bore little resemblance to any known language of antiquity, they were simply labeled forgeries.

How could the scholars of that day possibly have known that the Ancients wrote in what we today would consider a "strange language;" a language that both Ether and Mormon inform us could never be understood without the aid of divine interpreters. It is no wonder the scholastic world was so confused by them.

> And now, behold, we have written this record according to our knowledge, in the characters which are called among us the reformed Egyptian, being handed down and altered by us, according to our manner of speech.
>
> And if our plates had been sufficiently large we should have written in Hebrew; but the Hebrew hath been altered by us also; and if we could have written in Hebrew, behold, ye would have had no imperfection in our record.
>
> But the Lord knoweth the things which we have written, and also that none other people knoweth our language; and because that none other people knoweth our language, therefore he hath prepared means for the interpretation thereof. (Morm. 9:32–34)

Even the Prophet Joseph Smith needed the Seer Stones to translate the ancient plates entrusted to him by the Angel Moroni. Because these interpreters were not available to the world of Academia numerous tablets with strange inscriptions were simply dismissed as fraudulent—and often with no more than one quick glance.

~ ~ ~

Vast numbers of such relics were found and subsequently discarded in the lands surrounding Michigan. Henriette Mertz, in her impressive work, *The Mystic Symbol*, comments:

> Hundreds of objects—numbering even into the thousands—bore inscriptions in some strange writing containing characters which no one who examined them could either read or tell from what language they came. While the academic world remained inflexible, refusing to move from their position that all these artifacts had been forged, a

majority of unconvinced Michigan farmers, in turn, stubbornly refused to believe that anyone had trespassed on their land secreting this array of inexplicable material. To a farmer, that which he ploughed up was not "planted" on his land at any recent date regardless of whether or not it could be read.[5]

It appears that as early American colonists in Michigan and its surrounding territories began to clear their fields, numerous relics were unearthed, which, at first glance, were thought to belong to the loathsome aborigines. Since such artifacts were commonly thought to be worthless, most were simply discarded. However, because the curious inscriptions on many appeared to be of great antiquity, others were turned over to museums and antiquarians for further inspection. Unfortunately, it was not long before forged artifacts began to emerge. Even more unfortunate was the fact that once such fakes were discovered, the scholars of the day considered most

Calendar stone. Courtesy Museum of
Church History and Art, The Church of
Jesus Christ of Latter-day Saints.

other inscribed relics to be forgeries as well. Thus, a policy was established by the world of academia condemning all inscribed material as fraudulent. And, as each one appeared on the scene, it was summarily dismissed without further study.

Such an unprecedented atmosphere of distrust throughout American Academia began to concern notable men around the world, and thus, many determined to make their own evaluation. Not surprisingly, "several archeologists of international standing identified the objects as belonging to a civilization which many historians believe preceded that of the American Indians of this continent."[6] Even with such lofty appraisals, however, the whole affair caused such distaste in the scholastic world that any new relic discovered after that, no matter how intriguing, was either considered a fake or given little or no attention at all.

Unfortunately, the sentiments reflected by Francis W. Kelsey, Professor of Latin on the faculty of the University of Michigan, were the sentiments of far too many. In an article dated January 28, 1892, he makes his feelings public.

> Here is evidence then, of a deliberate and laborious attempt at imposition. . . . Is this the work of an unbalanced religious fanatic, for whom some prophet will arise in due time and interpret the supposed mystic symbol into a new creed?[7]

Could his antagonism be in direct response to the earlier story of a young man (Joseph Smith) who alleged to have been given custody of some golden plates, for a time, and who then translated them and organized a new religion? Unfortunately, because of such heated debates on the subject, far too many invaluable links to the past have been destroyed and are forever lost to us.

Those who believed in the authenticity of the relics, however, never lost hope. Over the years, hundreds of people testified that those they discovered were not forgeries, and numerous eye witnesses testified in their behalf. Even so, no one could even venture a guess at how they came to be buried in Michigan.

Mertz comments on the error of claiming so much fraud:

> It now appears that gross and serious error was committed by those into whose care these specimens were confided, thus resulting in irreparable loss. An academic group not recognizing the writing as having been set down in any letters with which they themselves were familiar, to save their self esteem, charged that it was fraudulent. They called attention to the writing which bore an unmistakable mixture of cuneiform, Egyptian hieroglyphs, Phoenician and Greek letters. Without hesitation and needing merely one quick glance, each and every professor agreed that the specimens were rank forgeries. And on that charge they stood unified and immovable.[8]

Several honorable men, such as Mr. Soper, Dean Savage, and Mr. Scotford, undaunted by such suspicions and out and out attacks on their honesty and integrity, continued to collect specimens over the years. Mounds were opened in full view of eye witnesses to avoid any claim of deception, and the relics found within were carefully catalogued and saved. While no special interest was ever given these astonishing relics during their lifetime, their collection of more than three thousand pro-

vide outstanding evidence that an ancient civilization with a superior culture once inhabited the region.

Because skepticism regarding the authenticity of the inscribed tablets found in Michigan existed for such a long time, and, in fact, are still being debated today, Henriette Mertz, a noted scholar with many years in pre-Columbian studies and professionally trained in forgery identification, was

Michigan Relic. Wayne May, *Ancient American Magazine.*

asked to inspect them in 1950. Mertz was a patent lawyer by profession, and was admitted to practice before the United States Supreme Court, the United States Patent Office, the Canadian Patent Office, and the Supreme Court of Illinois. Using the most modern methods available, she noted the Michigan Relics to be completely authentic. In fact, things which first appeared to be inconsistencies ultimately proved their authenticity. Every possible test was given. Alphabets and inscriptions from other ancient civilizations were used as study guides, legends and other information of historical relevance were utilized, and the time ascribed their beginnings was carefully studied. In fact, every modern method of forgery detection was used. The outcome was inevitable.

> When writing on these tablets was subjected to examination, as is customary in litigated cases involving forgery by this author, professionally qualified to examine questions of forgery, forgery was not found to exist. Analysis indicated that each individual tablet containing writing originated with a different hand. No two specimens examined produced identical characteristics—a humanly impossible feat if one person alone would have been guilty of forging the entire group of 3000. If these specimens belie forgery—and they do—then some 3000 inscribed specimens would indicate 3000 separate individuals created them and they therefore must be what they purport to be on their face.
>
> We then turned our attention to the drawings, finding both Old and New Testament stories indicating an intimate acquaintance with even the most trivial detail. . . .
>
> Writing proved to be authentic—not forged—and, subjected to decipherment, found to be written in abbreviated form on a vertical stem, a type common to the fourth century. When broken down into Greek alphabet letters words such as Lord, Master, Jesus, commingle with drawings representing Jesus, Lord and Master. Nothing appeared whether inconsistent or illogical—every unrelated subject examined. . . .

Fifteen specimens were submitted to me. Of the fifteen, no two had been written by the same hand—thus automatically eliminating the question of forgery by one person. The material is authentic.

In conclusion, as noted earlier, we believe the persons who inscribed this material were Christian refugees fleeing from Decian or Diocleclian persecutions and sailing out from the harbors of Rome, Naples, Alexandria, Carthage and other Eastern Mediterranean ports and assumed lost in the turbulent waters of the North Atlantic.[9]

Thus, by 1964, after every modern means of forgery detection was used by one eminently qualified to litigate cases of forgery before the courts, the Michigan Relics have been classified as completely authentic.

~ ~ ~

While Mertz's suggestion that Old World Christians fleeing from persecution may have authored the relics upon arrival in the New World seems perfectly reasonable, seeing as how the Lord does move his people around from time to time, especially in

Michigan Relic, showing two separate cultures. Wayne May, *Ancient American Magazine.*

times of great need, those familiar with the Book of Mormon might come up with another scenario altogether. We might reasonably suggest that since so many of these antiquities contained New Testament themes, the Nephites themselves may have authored the relics after the Savior's visit among them.

According to the most recent archeological findings, the origin of the Hopewell Culture, which was the more enlightened of the two mound building cultures and which most nearly matches the Nephite nation, was thought to have begun near the eastern end of Lake Ontario (New York). Now, the scriptures, inform us that rather large groups of Nephites left Zarahemla, from time to time, and migrated to other regions. Not surprisingly, archeological findings suggest the same things and follow the migration of various Hopewell from New York westward along the lower Great Lakes as far as Michigan. Thus, we can reasonably suggest that those who authored the Michigan Relics were a part of the over-all Nephite civilization; a people who had always been faithful in keeping their records.

~ ~ ~

Various scenes of daily life were found on the Michigan Relics. Some even showed elephants being used as beasts of

Davenport elephant pipe. Rendering from Charles E. Putman, *A Vindication of the Authenticity of the Elephant Pipes and Inscribed Tablets,* 1885.

burden—just as described in the scriptures. Unfortunately, this was just one more topic of contention during those early years, for the world of academia was totally convinced that, other than the more archaic Mastodon, elephants did not roam North America in ancient times. Moreover, they spent considerable time trying to disprove the authenticity of artifacts such as elephant pipes, which surfaced from time to time. However, the book of Ether clearly states the Jaredites were contemporary with the elephant.

> And they also had horses, and asses, and there were elephants and cureloms and cumoms; all of which were useful unto man, and more especially the elephants and cureloms and cumoms. (Ether 9:19)

Although we do not recognize those extinct animals called cureloms and cumoms, the elephant is readily recognized by those in our day. Whether they were a part of both the Nephite and Jaredite civilizations we have no way of knowing, for the scriptures only mention them in connection with the Jaredites. But, since they were well established in the land during the long Jaredite era it is completely possible, and perhaps probable, that they still roamed the land during the Nephite era as well. The Michigan tablets clearly suggest they did.

Others were also convinced these so called fabled beasts existed in America. In *The Mystic Symbol* we read:

> In 1951, elephant bones were recovered in Wisconsin, north east from Madison and, in 1959, elephant bones were recovered in Fulton County, Indiana, due south of South Bend. The latter find was immediately dismissed as being an "ice age" elephant. Without study of surrounding circumstances, one often wonders, along with Willy Ley, just what does happen in America today concerning elephant bones. Are they all, in fact, from the ice-age? Are they all mastodon? Must they again be re-buried so that we shall be forced to forget them-keeping an interested public ignorant of these finds? Illustrations of elephants appear on several of these Michigan tablets-elephants with ears typical of Southeastern Asia. Would it not be proper to enquire whether or not elephants had any connection with ancients who made their last stand at the Falls of the Ohio? Must we deny credibility to any picture that the academic community can not readily explain within the circumscribed sphere of their teaching?"[10]

If the Michigan Relics are genuine, and they have been proven to be so by a noted specialist in the field, then they provide added assurance that elephants did roam the land in times of antiquity. Of even more importance, however, is that they also support the premise that the northeast was inhabited by a white race (often decked out in helmets and breastplates), who lived a high order of civilization with a written language. It also shows evidence of another race (always decked out in plumed headdresses), who were often at war with the Michigan race.

~   ~   ~

Although a variety of themes are depicted on the Michigan

Relics, some of the most interesting depict religious themes. Obviously, artifacts with such themes are not unique to this area, for such pictographs can be found all over the world and reveal that people in all lands have a knowledge of the Great Flood, the Tower of Babel story, and the Creation. Yet, according to Mertz, of all the religious artifacts found in the Western Hemisphere the only ones depicting New Testament themes are found in North America on the Michigan Relics. While the Book of Mormon informs us that the Nephites

Noah and the Flood, showing gathering of animals, the Deluge, and disembarking. Wayne May, *Ancient American Magazine.*

were well acquainted with Old Testament stories, New Testament themes could only have been learned from the Savior himself after his own death and resurrection, for his mortal ministry occurred half way around the world from those in the New World. Thus, only after his visit to the Americas could such stories have been learned.

During that glorious time of enlightenment, the Savior taught the Nephites all things, from the beginning to the end of time, which they were then instructed to record. Surely the most precious story of his birth, life, and death would have been preserved in one form or another. Thus, not only were many historical episodes found on the Michigan tablets, but a treasury of religious instruction as well. Some tablets depict the Savior's birth, complete with shining star, while others, depict his life, and subsequent death upon the cross. Others depicted only God's singular watchful eye. Not surprisingly, each and every religious theme correlates beautifully with the scriptures.

~ ~ ~

Because of the on-going controversy regarding the authenticity of the Michigan Relics, even those in the Church have been understandably cautious about reaching any definite conclusion on the matter. Nonetheless, some have made their feelings known such as James Talmage, who personally examined about twenty pieces in 1911, and felt they were fraudulent. In his subsequent report on the matter he made the following statement, which, in light of more modern findings, is most interesting. He said: "If the objects brought together by Mr. Soper and Dean Savage were genuinely archaic, they would support the following statements:

1. "That the north-central area of the United States, more specifically the present State of Michigan, was inhabited in the long-ago, before the existence of the present tribal divisions of our North American Indians, by

a numerous people belonging to the Caucasian race and possessing a high degree of civilization.

2. "That, living at the same time and inhabiting the same area was another people of inferior culture, resembling the Indians of today both in physiognomy and customs.

3. "That these two people, representing widely different cultures were at enmity one with the other, and that the people of the higher class were in a state of constant migrations, seemingly fleeing before the assault of their semi-barbarous foes. . . .

4. "That the people of higher culture used a written language comprising both pictographic and other characters. None of these written characters had points of resemblance to the alphabets of the Orient, especially the Egyptian, the Greek, the Assyrian, the Phoenician, and the Hebrew.

5. "That the people of the higher class had a knowledge of certain books of Jewish scriptures, specifically Genesis, and possibly also later books belonging to the Old Testament compilation."[11]

~ ~ ~

Elder Milton R. Hunter, on the other hand, felt the tablets were authentic, and, in a letter to Mr. Ellis Clarke Soper, January 20, 1965, made the following comment:

Also, the fact that many people have proclaimed that both Father Savage's and your father's collections are frauds or forgeries makes your and my problem much more complicated.

As you know, I, personally, however, feel that the artifacts are all genuine.[12]

Although the controversy regarding the authenticity of the Michigan Relics continues both within and without of the church, modern methods of forgery detection, from at least one eminently qualified source, have declared them to be completely authentic.

While the authors of these relics still seem to mystify the scholastic world, it is estimated that over thirty thousand such relics have been found with both inscriptions and pictographs, which clearly indicate that a culture familiar with Egyptian traditions and with an understanding of the Hebrew religion once lived in the area. Thus, we have one more powerful piece of evidence that the northeast was populated by people who match the description of the Nephites and Lamanites perfectly.

Nonetheless, we should bear in mind that others besides the Nephites may have also been led to the promised land at some point in history, for the promised land was set aside to be a refuge for Christian-based societies. Could some of those who were fleeing the wholesale slaughter of Christians after the crucifixion of the Savior have been led to America just as the Nephites were led to her shores before the destruction of Jerusalem in 600 B.C.? Thus, even though the pictographs on the Michigan relics portray a people similar in fashion and culture to those of the Nephites and Lamanites, the possibility exists that they may just be another branch of Israel altogether.

~  ~  ~

Although a variety of themes are depicted on the relics, one of the most dominant is that of war; usually between a helmeted race of men who face an enemy wearing feathered headdresses. Some may question why so much warfare was depicted along with so many Christian themes, but we might remember, that war predominated both those years preceding the Nephite's golden era and those following. Thus, those relics which portray both Christian themes and warfare are perfectly compatible with the saga played out in the Book of Mormon. Therefore, whether the Michigan relics were made by a western branch of the Nephite nation or by other immigrants from the Old World, as suggested by Mertz, the inscribed tablets

Michigan Relic. Opposing armies show
two distinct cultures.
Wayne May, *Ancient American Magazine.*

found in Michigan clearly indicate that those who inscribed
them were familiar with the Savior's birth, life, and death—
just as the Book of Mormon informs us the Nephites were.

~  ~  ~

Interestingly, relics similar to those found in Michigan
have recently been discovered in the Burrows Cave in Illinois.
Now, if authentic, they give evidence that a people with perhaps
a Mediterranean background may have entered the land. Some
suggest mariners from the ports along the Mediterranean may

have led the Mulekites to their destination. Others suggest that certain mariners, upon hearing of the lucrative copper mines near Lake Superior, may have sailed across the sea and up the Mississippi to exploit the rich deposits in that region. Several such theories have been suggested. We must remember, however, that even if other cultures did enter the country at various points in history, they, too, must have turned from the ways of the Lord and were either destroyed or were driven from the land altogether, for only the Lamanites remained at the time of European contact. The edict by the Lord, God Almighty that only those who lived righteously would be permitted to remain in the promised land was an everlasting decree, and any who turned to wickedness, and refused to repent, would have been dealt with by the mighty hand of God.

> But he would that they should come forth even unto the land of promise, which was choice above all other lands, which the Lord God had preserved for a righteous people.
>
> And he had sworn in his wrath unto the brother of Jared, that whoso should possess this land of promise; from that time henceforth and forever, should serve him, the true and only God, or they should be swept off when the fulness of his wrath should come upon them. (Ether 2:7–8)

Since the Lamanites were the only ones in possession of the country at the time of European contact, we would have to assume that any who entered the land before that time were either destroyed at some point in history, became part of the Lamanite culture, or were driven completely away from the promised land rather than be allowed to defile it further. Many tales are yet to be told, but only when the records are restored will we know the whole and complete story of all those, both righteous and not, who lived and died in the mound building regions of the eastern woodlands.

~   ~   ~

## Notes

1. Roberts, *New Witness for God*, 52–53.
2. Ibid., 57.
3. Adair, *History of the American Indians*, 187.
4. Silverberg, *Mound Builders*, 76.
5. Mertz, *Mystic Symbol*, 2.
6. Ibid., 22.
7. Ibid., 14.
8. Ibid., 2.
9. Ibid., 48.
10. Ibid., 90.
11. Talmage, *Michigan Relics*.
12. Hunter to Soper, January 20, 1965.

Chapter Six

# Mounds and Enclosures

While debates on the authenticity of various relics filled news articles and lecture halls, mound exploration not only continued but intensified. Unfortunately, much of the raw data that filtered in was nothing more than a mish-mash of information gleaned from both lay men and professionals alike. Thus, by the middle of the 1800s it was becoming increasingly apparent that a more scientific approach to mound exploration was needed.

During those early years, it was common practice for curiosity seekers to desecrate ancient burial mounds and carry away relics by the arm loads. To add to the problem, treasure seekers were robbing the mounds and asking outrageous prices for their booty, which then spawned the unscrupulous practice of forgery. The entire atmosphere was one of confusion mixed with more than just a little skepticism regarding the mounds, their builders, and the treasures buried deep within them. Each new theory that surfaced added even more intrigue. Thus, the time was at hand for a more controlled investigation; one that would weed out any misinformation gleaned over the years in hopes of coming to some sort of agreement as to the origin of the Mound Builders and their various antiquities.

It was about this time that E. G. Squier came upon the scene. Squier was a newspaper editor and part-time politician who took a particular interest in the mounds. His approach to excavation and his detailed records, maps, and drawings won him the support of the American Ethnological Society, who not only encouraged his endeavors but gave him and his companion, Dr. E. H. Davis, a Chillicothe physician, their financial support as well. Together, Squier and Davis surveyed the mounds and prepared beautiful renderings of them, many of which are included in this body of work. Their comprehensive investigations have remained a basis for all succeeding archeological expeditions, and even though views regarding the mounds have changed somewhat over the years, their work is still respected today.

~ ~ ~

The search for answers to the mystery surrounding the mounds drove Squier and Davis through state after state, tirelessly studying each structure and its contents. They examined ancient forts and enclosures, climbed to the top of great earthen monuments and viewed numerous ancient burial sites—including the treasures interred in them. Then, after exhaustive research of the entire mound building region, they concluded the Mound Builders were indeed from a superior "vanished race." Moreover, Squier was completely convinced that no one who actually examined the ancient fortifications could come to any other conclusion. He said:

> The race, by whom these forts were erected, possessed no inconsiderable knowledge of the science of defense,—a degree of knowledge much superior to that known to have been possessed by hunter tribes of North America previous to the discovery by Columbus, or indeed subsequent to that event.[1]

He was also of the opinion that those who built the extensive network of mounds "spread southward, constantly developing itself in its progress," for he could trace their fortifications from western New York State through Ohio and into southern Illinois. He commented:

> The vast amount of labor necessary to the erection of most of these works precludes the notion they were hastily constructed to check a single or unexpected invasion. On the contrary, there seems to have existed a *System of Defenses* extending from the sources of the Allegheny and Susquehanna in New York, diagonally across the country, through central and northern Ohio, to the Wabash. Within this range, the works which are regarded as defensive are largest and most numerous. If an inference may be drawn from this fact, it is that the pressure of hostilities was from the northeast; or that, if the tide of migration flowed from the south, it received its final check upon this line. . . . We may suppose that from this direction came the hostile savage hordes, before whose incessant attacks the less warlike mound-builders gradually receded, or beneath whose exterminating cruelty those who occupied this frontier entirely disappeared, leaving these monuments alone to attest their existence, and the extraordinary skill with which they defended their altars and their homes. Upon either assumption, it is clear that the contest was a protracted one, and that the race of the mounds were for a long period constantly exposed to attack.

~ ~ ~

Squier and Davis's exhaustive research of the earthenworks in the region ultimately culminated in the large and beautifully illustrated book, *Ancient Monuments of the Mississippi Valley.* However, since the American Ethnology Society was unable to finance the work, it was published by the newer, wealthier Smithsonian Institution. Nonetheless, even after such extensive research Squier, too, joined the growing number of those who were still unable to explain the total and complete disappearance of the race of people known as the Mound Builders around A.D. 400. (Only the Book of Mormon holds that answer.)

~ ~ ~

As their explorations continued, Squier carefully sketched many of the ancient structures they examined in an effort to

preserve a record for posterity. He also drew their various shapes and sizes, for there were several different types. Most mounds were conical, but there were also flat topped pyramids and still others that resembled various animals. The latter of these mounds, or the effigy mounds as they were called, were found more to the west, in Michigan, Wisconsin, and Minnesota. They were made of clay and earth and

Great Serpent Mound. Squier and Davis, *Ancient Monuments,* 1848.

modeled after "otter, buffalo, snakes, lizards, turtles, bears, and other creatures." Although he was unable to discern whether they were made by outlying settlements belonging to the Ohio Mound Builders or by an entirely different culture altogether, he was saddened that they were quickly disappearing as modern settlements began to cover the land.

Squier also observed the conical mounds in the north were considerably different than the pyramidal structures found in the south. But, because he spent less time examining the southern mounds, he was reluctant to form an opinion of them other than to suggest they were either built by a totally different culture than the Mound Builders, or by those who were migrating southward from warring factions to the north.

~ ~ ~

Great Mound, Marietta, Ohio.
Squier and Davis, *Ancient Monuments,* 1848.

While the explorations of Squier and Davis took them throughout the entire mound building region, their most extensive surveys were made in the Ohio Valley where over ten thousand mounds were located. They felt their best chance of discovering the mysteries surrounding the mounds would be in this region, for the Ohio Valley seemed to be the center of the Mound Builder's civilization. As it turns out they were not far off in their suppositions, for the mounds in that region ultimately produced a treasury of ancient artifacts and a great deal of information regarding their builders.

As their investigation continued, Squier and Davis divided the various earthen works into two types, "mounds" and "enclosures." The "enclosures" were usually of two types, those they classified as "defensive" and those classified as "sacred." Both were bounded by embankments or walls and often incorporated many acres of land. Though many have long since been destroyed, thankfully others still exist, such as Fort Hill, in Highland County, Ohio, and Fort Ancient, in Warren County.

Squier was convinced that Fort Hill was constructed for military purposes and said:

It is quite unnecessary to recapitulate the features
which give to this the character of a military work; for they
are too obvious to escape attention. The angles of the hill
form natural bastions, enfilading the wall. The position of
the wall, the structure of the ditch, the peculiarities of the
gateways where ascent is practicable, the greater height of
the wall where the declinivity of the hill is less abrupt, the
reservoirs of water, the look-out citadel, all go to sustain
that conclusion.[2]

He felt that as a work of defense it was "well chosen,
well guarded, and with an adequate force was impregnable."
This type of fort was found in numerous areas, which convinced him that warfare was a big part of life for the Mound
Builders. (Just as it was in the Book of Mormon.)

~ ~ ~

One of the most impressive forts was found near Warren
County, Ohio and is known as Fort Ancient. Squier recorded:

It has not far from four miles of embankments, for the most
part very heavy, rising, at the more accessible points, to the
height of eighteen and twenty feet. . . . It occupies a terrace
on the left bank of the river, and two hundred and thirty feet
above its waters. The embankment stands 20 ft. high with
an outward slope of from "thirty five to forty-three
degrees." There is no ditch around it.

He was "astonished to see a work, simply of earth, after
braving the storms of thousands of years, still so entire and
well marked." Squier, noted several circumstances that contributed to this and recorded: "The clay of which it is built is
not easily penetrated by water. The bank has been, and is still
mostly covered by a forest of beech trees, which have woven
a strong web of their roots over its steep side; and a fine bed
of moss serves still further to afford protection."[3] He comments further:

A review of this magnificent monument cannot fail
to impress us with admiration of the skill which selected,

and the industry which secured this position. Under a military system, such as we feel warranted in ascribing to the people by whom this work was constructed, it must have been impregnable. In every point of view, it is certainly one of the most interesting remains of antiquity which the continent affords.[4]

The defensive enclosures amazed all who gazed upon them. Nadaillac, in his *Pre-Historic America,* said:

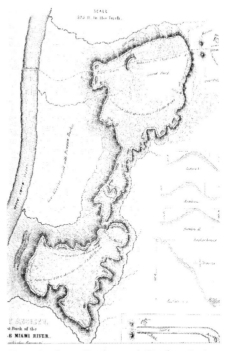

Fort Ancient. Squier and Davis, *Ancient Monuments,* 1848.

> These works bear witness to the intelligence of the race, which has so long been looked upon as completely barbarous and wild, and an actual system of defenses in connection with each other can in some cases be made out with observatories on adjacent heights, and concentric ridges of earth for the protection of the entrances. War was evidently an important subject of thought with the Mound Builders. All the defensive remains occur in the neighborhood of water courses, and the best proof of the skill shown in the choice of sites is shown by the number of flourishing cities, such as Cincinnati, St. Louis, Newark, Portsmouth, Frankfort, New Madrid, and many others, which have risen in the same situations in modern times.[5]

~ ~ ~

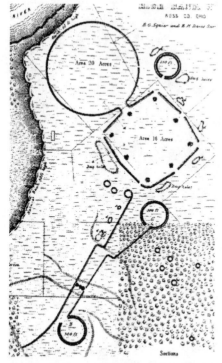

Ancient works at High Banks, Ohio. Squier and Davis, *Ancient Monuments,* 1848.

Although the enclosures built for defense were particularly intriguing to Squier and Davis, still other types were found as well, such as those thought to be sacred in nature. These enclosures were far less imposing than those built for defense and were most commonly built along the broad level river bottoms, rather than upon table lands or where the surface of the ground was not especially even. They were most often found in groups and were usually square or circular with "a nearly uniform diameter of two hundred and fifty or three hundred feet, with a ditch interior to the wall."[6]

The smaller circles were occasionally found within larger works of a different character. The larger circles were often found in combination with the rectangular and were connected to them either directly or by avenues. Some took in fifty or more acres.

Squier also noticed that certain groups were marked by a great uniformity of size noting that five or six in the area were exact squares, "each measuring one thousand and eighty feet," a coincidence which Squier noted "could not possibly be accidental, and which "must possess some significance." He further commented that "this certainly establishes the extent of some standard of measurement among the ancient people, if not the possession of some means of determining angles."[7] He noted further that, "these figures are not only accurate squares and prefect circles, but are in most cases of corresponding dimensions, that is to say, the sides of each of the squares are each ten hundred and eighty feet in length; and the diameter of each of the large and small circles, a fraction over seventeen hundred and eight hundred feet, respectively."[8]

Squier was also impressed with the great extent of some of the enclosures and makes special note of one of considerable size near Newark, Ohio.

> Another class of works, probably akin to those here noticed, are the parallels, consisting of slight embankments seven or eight hundred feet in length and sixty or eighty feet apart. Indeed, so various are these works, and so numerous their combinations, that it is impossible, through the medium of description alone, to convey an adequate conception of their character. If we are right in the assumption that they are of sacred origin, and were the temples and consecrated grounds of the ancient people, we can, from their number and extent, form some estimate of the devotional fervor or superstitious zeal which induced their erection, and the predominance of the religious sentiment among their builders.
>
> There magnitude is, perhaps, the strongest objection that can be urged against the purpose here assigned them. It is difficult to comprehend the existence of religious works, extending, with their attendant avenues, like those near Newark, over an area of little less than four square miles. We can find their parallels only in the great temples of Abury and Stonehenge in England and Carnac in Brittany, and must associate them with sun worship and its kindred superstitions.[9]

~ ~ ~

The enclosures, both defensive and sacred, were particularly intriguing to Squier and Davis, but the mounds were far more numerous and they, too, needed investigating. So, up and down the mounds they tramped, measuring, surveying and investigating both their contents and their surroundings. After much attention was given to every possible detail, the mounds were ultimately classified into four categories: 1. Altar Mounds, 2. Burial Mounds, 3. Temple Mounds, and 4. Anomalous Mounds.

It seems the Altar Mounds occurred within enclosures or in the near vicinity. They were stratified, and contained altars of burned clay or stone, which led many to believe they were places of sacrifice.

The Temple Mounds, which were also found within an enclosure, but not always, contained neither altars nor human remains. Squier considered them "High Places" used for religious ceremonies.

Burial Mounds were found in all regions. These were the mounds Squier knew the best, and he commented:

> Within these mounds, we must look for the only authentic remains of their builders. They are the principal depositories of ancient art; they cover the bones of the distinguished dead of remote ages; and hide from the profane gaze of invading races the altars of the ancient people.

The mounds set aside for burial are by far the most numerous of all the mounds. They vary in size from six to eighty six feet in height but usually average between fifteen to twenty five feet. For the most part, they are not located within the walls of enclosures but are usually found at some distance from them. Sometimes they stand completely alone and at other times they can be found in clusters which may indicate a certain connection between those interred. They have no altars and are usually conical in shape, although they can also be elliptical or pear-shaped.

Most authorities agree that burial mounds were not intended for the general populations but were most likely created to inter the more noble members of the area, perhaps chieftains or other distinguished people. It has been difficult to determine where the masses have been buried because cremation was such a big part of the ancient burial customs. Silverberg suggests that as much as three-fourths of their total

Burial mounds. Squier and Davis, *Ancient Monuments,* 1848.

population was cremated, with tomb burials reserved for the high caste among them. Squier even suggested that some mounds may have been composed of the ashes of the honored dead. But the fact that many were simply buried beneath the earth is evidenced by the great number of skeletons that have washed ashore as rivers flooded or changed course over the years.

The Anomalous Mounds, were simply those that did not fall within the other three categories or their purpose was not readily understood. It was from these various mounds and enclosures that we gleaned all the information we currently have about the ancient architects of these magnificent works.

Although on-going explorations and surveys of the mounds continued to bring more and more information to light, the subject of the origin of the Mound Builders was still considered a complete mystery. B. H. Roberts in *New Witness for God,* commented:

> Concerning the matter of the Mound Builders in general we are again in the presence of a subject concerning which there is very great diversity of opinions on the part of authorities. Learned opinion is divided as to whether the mounds represent an indigenous or exotic civilization; whether they were built by the ancestors of the near or

remote Indian tribes of North America, or by a race now extinct or by some mysterious process or other, "vanished." Also they differ as to the antiquity of the mounds, some ascribing them to quite a recent origin, and others ascribing them to an antiquity of thousands of years.[10]

As each new theory arose it was carefully studied, debated and usually discarded, which led Samuel F. Haven, the librarian of the American Antiquarian Society, to conclude, "none have led to a satisfactory solution."[11]

And so the debate continued on and on and back and forth throughout the remainder of the nineteenth century, with the two main theories predominating; one that the ancient ancestors of the Indians had built the mounds, and, the other, that a "lost race" had erected them—and neither side was willing to concede to the other.

~ ~ ~

## Notes

1. Squire, *Antiquities of the State of New York,* 303.

2. Squier and Davis, *Ancient Monuments of the Mississippi Valley,* 16.

3. Ibid., 20.

4. Ibid., 21.

5. Nadaillac, *Pre-Historic America,* 88.

6. Squire and Davis, *Ancient Monuments of the Mississippi Valley,* 48.

7. Ibid., 48–49.

8. Ibid., 56.

9. Ibid., 49.

10. Roberts, *New Witness for God,* 1:453.

11. Silverberg, *Mound Builders,* 98.

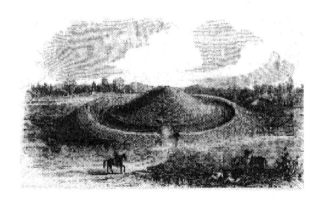

Chapter Seven

# The Debate Thickens

When the extensive surveys and explorations of Squier and Davis were published in the large, beautifully illustrated work, *Ancient Monuments of the Mississippi Valley,* in 1848, even more interest in mound excavation was generated. Archeological explorations were taking place world wide at this point in history, and discoveries of great importance were capturing the attention of people everywhere. Tombs of the Pharaohs were being opened, and the ruins of magnificent cities were being discovered in many lands. Charles Darwin's theory of evolution recently entered the picture as well, and efforts to equate the skulls of seemingly prehistoric men with his theory was a favorite topic of discussion among both lay-men and scholars alike. To add to that spirit of excitement, the recent tale of Joseph Smith and certain golden tablets, which supposedly held answers regarding the ancient inhabitants of the region, added even more intrigue. Unfortunately, by this time, so many theories had already been postulated that no one took this theory any more seriously than any others. (Other than those who, touched by the Spirit, recognized the truth of it.)

As late as the close of the 1800s, interest in mound exploration was still rather high, but as towns and cities began to spread across the land and pioneers began to migrate westward, interest in the mounds in general began to fade. Moreover, the on-going debate about their builders had spawned such controversy over the preceding two centuries, that the public was beginning to wonder just who and what to believe any more. Consequently, guards were up and caution about believing everything that came out in print was becoming the norm for the day. B. H. Roberts comments on that subject in *New Witness for God*:

> In considering authorities upon American antiquities, one thing should be especially observed: one should be upon his guard against the credulity and bias of the early writers; and equally upon his guard against the skepticism and bias of the more modern ones. The former, living in an age of superstition and credulity, and having special interests to serve, would have us believe too much; the latter, living in an age super-critical and doubting, would have us believe too little.[1]

Such comments were certainly not unfounded, for debates and arguments raged on year after year with neither side even the least bit inclined to concede to the other's point of view, even when ample evidence pointed in that direction. A true war of ideas was being waged with each side determined to come out the victor; one attributing the mounds to a lost race of enlightened people and the other to the ancestors of the Indians.

As popular as these theories were, in 1834, John Wesley Powell, who was born in Palmyra, New York near where Joseph Smith was given charge of the golden plates, began the self appointed task of discouraging the popular notion that a "superior lost race" once lived in the region. Powell was tutored about the mounds as a boy and enjoyed excavating those in Chillicothe where he found a few artifacts of his own. But, as his own personal excavations continued, he became more and more convinced the prevailing notion of a "lost race" was simply not a valid one, for some mounds contained both iron implements and glass beads. Thus, Powell was convinced that "at least some" of the artifacts found in the mounds had been created subsequent to the advent of the white man, and not by some "vanished race" as so many had supposed.

In later years, Powell became director of the Bureau of American Ethnology, which was a department of the Smithsonian Institution. Soon after, an immense book on the Indian nations was produced. But, as Silverberg pointed out, of its 638 pages, only eight were devoted to the mounds, for Powell felt there was absolutely no reason to search for a lost race of Mound Builders when the mounds appear "quite clearly to be the work of the ancestors of the modern Indians." Thus, it seemed that "battle lines were drawn" in the on-going debate over the authors of the various earthen works found throughout the countryside.

Now, although Powell helped escalate the war of ideas regarding the origin of the Mound Builders, it would be Cyrus Thomas, a botanist and geologist working for the Bureau, who made the greatest effort to debunk the lost race theory. In an early writing "he denounces 'the many false statements' and the 'contradictions and absurdities,' and asserts that the 'garbling and perversion of the lower class of writers supplemented the fantasies of those better intended."[2] And so began a systematic effort to discount all previously held theories while trying as best he could to supplant those theories with his own.

Under the auspices of the Bureau, Thomas began to question even those who had preceded the Bureau's own archeological research, commenting that the "researchers who have hitherto conducted the researches . . . were swept away by blind zeal into serious errors even when they were not imposed upon by frauds and forgeries." He even questioned the well respected work of Squier and Davis, suggesting they had been "too imaginative" in their interpretation of the animal effigy seen on a carved pipe. He was also skeptical of their supposition that the geometrical talents of the Mound Builders showed them to be of an advanced culture. Interestingly, his own findings would later prove the Ohio enclosures were geometrically perfect after all.

Nonetheless, in response to the continuing controversy and the growing number of theories being postulated, the Bureau, in spite of their own bias on the matter, made a renewed effort to investigate the mounds near the close of the 1800s. Not only did they hope a more scientific approach to mound exploration would help dispel the myths and fables associated with the Mound Builders, but they also had hopes of coming up with a satisfactory conclusion to the entire matter. Thus, the most comprehensive investigation of the mound regions of the eastern woodlands began, and with it, the beginning of the end of the more romantic notions of the past.

By 1883, Thomas had several assistants, and mound excavation began full time. Some 4,100 artifacts were unearthed during that time, but because a few were of obvious European origin it served to back Powell's original belief "that although some of the burial mounds of this district must be attributed to the so-called 'veritable mound-builders,' others were undoubtedly built by the Indians found inhabiting it at the advent of the whites." [3]

~ ~ ~

(Although some artifacts found in the mounds were of obvious European origins, not all questionable relics should be attributed to foreigners. Some thought glass could not have been known to the ancients and, therefore, concluded all glass artifacts must have come from Europe. We must remember, however, that even the brother of Jared had a knowledge of glass, else why would he have made reference to the sixteen small stones that were "as transparent as glass" (see Ether 3:1). Since this amazing experience took place shortly after the Universal Flood, there should be no hesitancy in attributing glass to those civilizations that peopled the region during the mound building era. And, likewise, iron, for the scriptures make it perfectly clear that the art of making steel weapons was well known by both the Nephites and the Jaredites. In fact, in speaking of pieces of cast iron found in New York, B. H. Roberts commented,"these articles cannot well be ascribed to the era of the French war, as time enough since, then, till the region round about Onondaga was commenced to be cultivated, had not elapsed to give the growth of timber found on the spot."[4] Thus, not all iron artifacts should be automatically relegated to a European origin simply because it appeared to be a work superior to the abilities of any known Indian tribe.)

~ ~ ~

In spite of Thomas' new thrust to discredit the lost race theory and to reconcile the builders of the mounds with the Indians, new theories continued to surface, such as one that credited the mounds to the survivors of the lost continent of Atlantis. Another equated the Mound Builders with the Toltecs, who, it was thought, after living in the region for a while, migrated southward into Mexico. Others thought the Aztecs were the Mound Builders. Nonetheless, many, including such men as Henry Schoolcraft, Dr. Haven and Sir John Lubbock, followed Thomas's lead in attributing the mounds to the Indians.[5] Nadaillac, too, joined that school of thought but, reminded us in his *Pre-Historic America,* that the ancestors of the modern Indians may well have been superior to their more nomadic descendants:

> It should, however, be distinctly understood that the reference to 'Indian' in connection with the mounds is a

strictly general term. The richest, most cultured, and most sedentary of the Indian tribes existing when the white race poured into America like a restless flood, have been destroyed; of many tribes none remain. Of others only a most feeble remnant exists or lately existed in a region to which they have been exiled from the lands of their fathers. Those who constitute the greater portion of our Indian population today are mere nomads, wanderers, the Bedouins of America, the idle wanderers who were not tied to the soil by their progress in culture, and who probably never troubled themselves about mounds as long as they could shift their wigwams from one good hunting ground to another. It is of these that one thinks as Indians when the contrast between Mound Builder and Indian is mooted.[6]

Thus, back and forth the debate continued, with one person of high standing relegating the mounds to one origin and someone else with similar credentials relegating them to yet another.

While Thomas continued to push for a resolution to the matter, a new theory arose in 1888, put forth by Frederick W. Putnam, curator of Harvard's Peabody Museum. Although he clearly did not accept most of the more exotic theories of the day, he was, nonetheless, of the opinion the Mound Builders were of a higher culture than the nomadic Indians, suggesting that "instead of a single race, there were a succession of mound-building races in the Ohio Valley."[7] This new hypothesis would prove to be a most important link in finding a solution to the matter, for, as students of the Book of Mormon will readily recognize, more than one culture did occupy the territory in the far distant past (both the Nephites and Lamanites, with the Jaredites occupying the region prior to that time).

~ ~ ~

Unresolved questions such as those regarding the origin of the Mound Builders, often lead thinking men and women into the realm of speculation in the on-going quest for truth. Unfortunately, unsuspected detours often lead them in circles around the truth before the answers finally come. Such would be the case in the search for the builders of the mounds, for although evidence was mounting that a race of superior beings were a part of the mound building epoch, by the end of the 1800s that theory was about to be discarded for a time, along with numerous other fanciful theories of the day.

The final blow to the "lost race" theory, although not fatal, came about in the late 1800s. Major J. W. Powell, conqueror of the Colorado River and founder of the Smithsonian Institution's Bureau of American Ethnology, who by this time was completely disgusted with the continuing debates on the subject, put forth his own strong views on the matter in an effort to dispel any lingering notions that a "lost race" had built the mounds, for he was totally convinced the Indians had built them and no one else.

Thomas explains the popular feelings of so many in regards to the lost race theory in the following statement:

> It is difficult to exaggerate . . . the force with which the hypothetic "lost races" had taken possession of the imaginations of men. For more than a century the ghosts of a vanished nation have ambuscaded in the vast solitudes of the continent, and the forest covered mounds have usually been regarded as the mysterious sepulchers of its kings and nobles. It was an alluring conjecture that a powerful people, superior to the Indians, once occupied the valley of the Ohio and the Appalachian ranges, their empire stretching from Hudson bay to the Gulf, with its flanks on the western prairies and the eastern ocean; a people with a confederated government, a chief ruler, a great central capital, a highly developed religion . . . all swept away before an invasion of copper-hued Huns from some unknown region of the earth, prior to the landing of Columbus.[8]

In 1894, Thomas finally completed the Bureau's twelfth and final 750-page report on the Mound Builders. Not surprisingly, his conclusion on the matter of the Mound Builders had not been altered at all. He was still totally convinced, and recorded such, that the mounds had been authored by the ancestors of the modern Indians and no one else. In that report we read:

> It is proper to state at this point, however, that the author believes the theory which attributes these works to the Indians (using the term in the limited sense heretofore explained) to be the correct one. . . . . He attributes all the ancient artificial works found in the Mississippi valley and Gulf states, or in that part of the United States east of the Rocky mountains, to the Indian tribes found in possession of this region at the time of its discovery, and their ancestors.[9]

In this impressive body of work, Thomas meticulously details each and every mound exploration undertaken by the Bureau, and recapped the various theories he supposedly overturned. However, as Silverberg observed: "Thomas' effort to deflate the myth led him to go too far in the opposite direction." Nonetheless, his monumental report was a culmination of such exhaustive research that it proved to many that the mounds and various earthen enclosures in the region belonged to the family of the American Indians, just as he had suggested. Thus, as Silverberg noted, the Bureau's lengthy report "marked the end of an era. No longer could one speak of 'the mound builders' in quite the same way, as masters of a vast empire." Moreover, he believed that, "Thomas had raised as many questions as he had answered," and that "his work was not so much an epilogue as a prologue."[14]

The whole matter had been debated for such a long time that when the report finally came out, the public simply accepted it without further arguments. They were undeniably disappointed, however, for if, the ancestors of the modern Indians had built the mounds, then the mystery, the romance, in fact the life's blood of the very quest itself completely lost its appeal, for the common ordinary Indians were of absolutely no interest to them at all. Thus, as towns and cities filled up the country and people began to be caught up in home, family and the various political intrigues of the day, the mounds slowly slipped out of the public's consciousness and have attracted little attention since.

In concluding his own impressive work, *The Mound Builders,* Silverberg makes the interesting and pertinent comment:

> It is difficult now to understand how intensely interested people were in the mounds and their builders a century and more ago, and we have trouble realizing why people were so eager to believe that the mounds were the creations of superior beings hidden in the mists of time. The old myths are dead, and archeologists smile at the fancies of yesteryear.
>
> Yet there is magic in the mounds even now. Forget the labors of Cyrus Thomas and other debunkers; . . . and all the other archeologists who have shown us why we must not think the builders of the mounds as the Mound Builders. Stand in the midst of the Newark octagon on a summer afternoon, or walk along Fort Ancient's wall, or scramble to the top of Cahokia, or look down from the observation tower upon Great Serpent Mound. All is green and silent; and, looking about at these mysterious grassy monuments, one surrenders easily to fantasy, and feels the presence of the ghosts of departed greatness, and then, in warm understanding, one reaches out across the decades to the makers of the Mound Builder myth.[10]

Thus, by the end of the 1800s the subject of the mounds and their builders were put to rest and little has been heard of them since.

~  ~  ~

Without the scriptures to rely on it is no wonder such debates continued for such a long time, for evidence of Indian occupation throughout the years, including during the mound building epoch, is simply overwhelming. Yet, evidence that a superior culture once occupied the region is also overwhelming. The scientific world was simply unable to reconcile these two facts during the eighteenth and nineteenth centuries. Fortunately, the archeological research done in the twentieth century has done much to clarify the issue.

While views have changed somewhat over the years, we must be cautious of discounting all earlier research, for discoveries made by both amateurs and those associated with the Bureau of Ethnology came up with impressive amounts of information regarding the mounds and their builders. Numerous earthen monuments were excavated, bones were examined and various antiquities were carefully analyzed in the ongoing effort to come to some conclusion on the matter. Thus, much has been gleaned over the years in regard to the life and times of that ancient people.

Dr. Bradford sums up much of the information accumulated at this point in time and concludes:

The Mound Builders

1. "were all of the same origin, branches of the same race, and possessed of similar customs and institutions.

2. "That they were populous, and occupied a great extent of territory.

3. "That they had arrived at a considerable degree of civilization, were associated in large communities, and lived in extensive cities.

4. "That they possessed the use of many of the metals such as lead, copper, gold, and silver, and probably the art of working in them.

5. "That they sculptured in stone, and sometimes used that material in the construction of their edifices.

6. "That they had the knowledge of the arch of receding steps; of the art of pottery—producing utensils and urns forged with taste, and constructed upon the principles of chemical compositions and of the art of brick-making.

7. "That they worked the salt springs, and manufactured that substance.

8. "That they were an agricultural people living under the influence and protection of regular forms of government.

9. "That they possessed a decided system of religion, and a mythology connected with astronomy, which, with its sister science geometry, was in the hands of the priesthood.

10. "That they were skilled in the art of fortification.

11. "That the epoch of their original settlement, in the United States, is of great antiquity."[11]

~ ~ ~

Now, since these points can also be equated with the Nephites, they lend further credence to the Book of Mormon's reference to an enlightened race of people who lived in the regions of the Hill Cumorah between 600 B.C.–A.D. 400; a nation which consisted of both an enlightened race, (the Nephites), and one resembling the aboriginal Americans found occupying the country at the time of European contact, (the Lamanites).

In spite of, or perhaps "because" of the debates that raged back and forth between scholars, archeologist, anthropologist and men of renown, the search for answers to support their various theories produced a treasury of information; information which provides ample evidence that the Mound Builders and the Nephite Nation were one and the same. In fact, discoveries too numerous to mention support the premise that the Book of Mormon lands were indeed located in the eastern woodlands of the United States; the artifacts found, the legends told, the traditions held sacred by all Indian Nations provide ample evidence that the Mound Builders were those very people whose history is played out in the Book of Mormon.

Nonetheless, such evidence would lack strength without a confirmation that the geography of the region also fits the descriptions of lands and places described within the scriptures. Therefore, we must expand the quest to include a geographical study of the region, for only by doing so we will discover whether or not the distribution of those lands described within the scriptures matches the regions of the eastern woodlands. Only by finding both archeological and geographical evidence in support of our claims can we be safe in our quest for a correlation between the Mound Builders and the Book of Mormon.

~ ~ ~

## Notes

1. Roberts, *New Witness for God*, 2:413.
2. Silverberg, *Mound Builders*, 132.
3. Thomas, *12th Annual Report of the Bureau of Ethnology*, 708.
4. Roberts, *New Witness for God*, 2:70.
5. Thomas, *12th Annual Report of the Bureau of Ethnology*, 600.
6. Nadaillac, *Pre-Historic America*, 186–87.
7. Silverberg, *Mound Builders*, 150.
8. Thomas, *12th Annual Report of the Bureau of Ethnology*, xli.
9. Ibid., 610.
10. Silverberg, *Mound Builders*, 266.
11. McGavin and Bean, *The Geography of the Book of Mormon*, 68, quoting Bradford, *American Antiquities*, 60–70.

Chapter Eight

# The Cumorah Lands

The mound building civilization, which has been dated to between 1000–500 B.C. and A.D. 400–500, was comprised of independent villages and cities which were dotted all across the eastern woodlands. Much of its population dominated the Ohio valley with other pockets filling up regions along the Mississippi, Missouri, and Illinois Rivers. Yet modern authorities such as Prufer and Dragoo believe this civilization had its origins in New York before spreading into other territories. Since mounting evidence indicates the Mound Builders and the Nephites were one and the same, and since the only known landmark we have is in New York (the Hill Cumorah), this must be the place to begin our search for the elusive lands of the Book of Mormon.

While archeological research indicates this culture eventually populated a rather large area, the scriptures indicate the saga played out in the Book of Mormon took place in a very limited region; a region not much bigger than the Bible Lands in the Old World, which took in only about 150 miles in length by half that size in width. Thus, a region the size of New York is not out of line. Although much of New York can safely be considered Book of Mormon territory, the greater challenge will be to locate the region where the greatest amount of activity took place—Zarahemla, or the "land southward." Now, isolating that region would be next to impossible without the numerous geographical descriptions found scattered throughout the scriptures. But, with that body of work before us, we can formulate a geographical picture that will help immensely in our search for the lost lands of the Book of Mormon, for it is important that we discover just how much of the woodlands actually made up Nephite territory.

Most Book of Mormon scholars now readily recognize that the "land southward," which included the lands of Bountiful, Zarahemla and Nephi, and is where most of the history contained in the Book of Mormon took place, was not a very large region. This reasoning is based on a number of facts, one of which is that Bountiful, the northernmost land in the "land southward," was described as being "only" one and a half day's journey wide: a journey that once measured would give us the approximate distance across Bountiful. Obviously, how long it would take one to travel that distance is best determined by those who have actually walked the region, such as Walter Pidgeon, who traveled nine hundred miles through the woodlands and recorded he made about twenty miles a day. This would gives us one estimate, but those who fought in the French and Indian war often did well to cover just three to six miles a day through the heavily forested regions of New York. Moreover, in O. Turner's *Pioneer History of the Holland Purchase of Western New York,* we read of men who traversed such rugged terrain that it took them two full days to travel just eight miles. But, since the time traveled is totally dependent on the terrain being traveled, and since the scriptures do not indicate that Bountiful was particularly mountainous or rugged, we can comfortably take the larger of the numbers, that of twenty miles. Even by taking the larger number, however, the land of Bountiful would still be only about thirty miles wide. Thus, it becomes readily apparent that Bountiful, which the scriptures tell us went from the east to the west sea, was not a great distance across. Moreover, since the scriptures tell us that Zarahemla lay just to the south of Bountiful with the land of Nephi just to the south of that, and considering all three lands were described as bordering the same east and west seas, we would have to assume they were all not much more than one and a half to three day's journey wide, depending on the course of the seas on either side. Thus, the land southward could not possibly have been very large.

The scriptures also describe this small region as being nearly surrounded by water. This single fact alone has been a stumbling block for many, for such waters do not present themselves in the modern New York setting. But, by going back to more ancient times, we can find water to the north, east, south and west of Cattaraugus and Erie Counties just to the east of Lake Erie in southwestern New York. Thus, this region may well have been the land southward during Book of Mormon times, for this small island of sorts was also only about one and a half to three day's journey wide during that distant era.

It is not enough to come up with a likely site for Zarahemla or Bountiful or this city or that, for each and every scriptural description must correlate perfectly with each and every other scriptural description if we are to find a legitimate location for the elusive lands of the Book of Mormon. For example, there must be every sea mentioned, a definable eastern border, a sea that divided the land southward from the land northward, a narrow neck of land, which provided a passageway from one side of the sea to the other, and a route leading to both the Hill Cumorah and to a land of many waters. There must also be hills and valleys to correlate the various ups and downs described in the scriptures. There must be a dividing line of sorts between the land of Nephi and the land of Zarahemla (such as the impressive gorge carved out by the waters of the Cattaraugus Creek, which runs from east to west across the land just to the east of Lake Erie). There must also be a river which traveled northward through Zarahemla and exited into a sea, (Buffalo River/Creek)and a place between the land of Nephi and the land of Zarahemla where the headwaters of that river could easily be crossed. There are many such geographical guidelines to consider in locating a region that meets all the requirements necessary to be the actual homeland of the Nephites and Jaredites. Furthermore, each and every piece of the puzzle must fit together perfectly, not just a few.

In this author's *The Lost Lands of the Book of Mormon,* this challenge has been met, with the land southward occupying the regions of southwestern New York and the land northward filling up those regions bordering Lake Ontario further to the north. Moreover, the land of many waters can successfully be equated with the beautiful Finger Lakes region, which consists of an expansive region just to the south of the Hill Cumorah, with that sacred hill sitting just under 100 miles from Zarahemla. Thus, the Cumorah lands were compact enough to permit those who were given the important charge of recording their histories to reasonably do so, for the means of travel and communication between lands and cities was certainly not like it is today.

Other evidences to support the premise the territory was rather small is that during the Jaredite era, the Prophet Ether was able to personally observe the battles of complete destruction during the final days of that nation's history. And during the Nephite era, those living in the south of Zarahemla could travel through the heavily forested "wilderness side" and reach cities in the northern regions in just three days. Moreover, those journeying from the cities in the southeastern borders could reach Bountiful, to the north, in just one day, which clearly indicates the entire territory was not very large. The over-all region was apparently small enough to allow fellow citizens to help build and protect one another's properties and cities on a regular basis, even though they were seemingly spread all across the land.

Obviously, this small territory did not contain the entire Nephite or Lamanite population, for the scriptures tell us many left their homeland from time to time and began to populate regions beyond the bounds of Book of

Book of Mormon territory.

Mormon territory. Thus, only the limited regions of western New York can rightly be described as the territory occupied by those whose history is contained in the Book of Mormon.

By way of example; if we were to take an aerial photo of the eastern half of the country and create a giant puzzle of that region, perhaps with each puzzle piece the size of our modern day states, the state of New York would be the piece that contains the saga of those whose history is contained in the Book of Mormon, with each of the other puzzle pieces having their own recorded history.

If we were to give it even more thought, we might realize how impossible it would be for one person to record the history of even one individual state. With millions occupying New York City alone, and several million more populating hundreds of cities scattered all across the state, it would be absolutely impossible to accomplish such a task, even today. Thus, the Lord, in his wisdom, instructed people in each region to keep their own records. Consequently, only the limited territory known as the land southward, with only a mere mention of those who migrated into the land northward, were recorded on the sacred plates.

While the scriptures give us an historical account of those occupying Book of Mormon territory, the archeological evidence amassed over the years gives us the most information regarding those who migrated into other regions, including their routes of migration. Cyrus Thomas of the Smithsonian's Bureau of Ethnology, for example, concluded their chief line of former occupancy is one that "reaches from New York through Ohio along the Ohio river and onward."[1] Thus, Thomas himself declared the origin of the Mound Building civilization had roots in New York state. Upon examining these regions, he found the works in New York were "found chiefly about the lakes," while those in Ohio were chiefly in the interior and southwestern part of the state, with the exception of a number in the northeast near Lake Erie."[2] He discounts the notion that they were one united nation, however, and said:

> The idea of one great nation is very fascinating, but the facts and reason are against it. If allowed to have their due weight on our minds, they must lead us to the more prosaic conclusion that the mound-builders were divided into different tribes and peoples, which, though occupying much the same position in the culture scale, and hence resembling each other in many of the habits, customs, and modes of life, were as widely separated in regard to their ethnic relations and languages as the Indian tribes when first encountered by the white races.[3]

Both archeological and scriptural accounts validate this supposition, for although both the Nephites and Lamanites originated from the same family unit, dissensions among them created divisions in the family that could never be repaired. Consequently, as disputes among them increased, the Nephites, who at first may have settled in the fertile regions of upper Ohio after possibly coming up the Mississippi and Ohio Rivers, migrated further northward into New York, while the Lamanites migrated southward along the Ohio River and settled in central and southern Ohio. Even so, the Lamanites continued to war with their Nephite brethren, pushing them further and further northward.

~ ~ ~

Now, because the warring Lamanites lay to the south of Zarahemla and because the land southward was nearly surrounded by water during that ancient era, those fleeing from Lamanite aggression were forced to travel northward through ancient Lake Tonawanda (the sea that divides the lands), which at one time lay in the plains just to the south of Lake Ontario. Once they passed through this ancient body of water (by way of a narrow neck of land, which extended from north to south right through the seabed,) they were then free to spread out along those northern regions bordering Lake Ontario, a safer distance from the Lamanites who were now separated from them by water. From there they could also move into the highly desirable

Nephite and Lamanite territory.

"land of many waters" (the Finger Lakes region). How far they may have migrated eastward through the Mohawk Valley and into the Eastern Seaboard we have no record, but there is archeological evidence that they also spread westward, skirting Lamanite territory and occupying those highly prized regions that bordered the various Great Lakes. (The earthen works in those areas are similar to those in New York. The bone pits are similar as well which strongly suggests the same culture, or one similar, occupied those territories.)

~ ~ ~

Because the lands of western New York match in every way the geographical descriptions of Book of Mormon territory, it should be no surprise to discover that the archeological findings from that region are also a perfect match. Remnants of fortified villages and towns just like those described in the scriptures dot the entire countryside, and artifacts of war have been found by the thousands, which indicates that great and terrible wars raged throughout the land at one time.

Not surprisingly, the greatest concentration of such artifacts have been found around the Hill Cumorah. The second greatest concentration of relics have been found in Erie County, that territory just to the east of Lake Erie. Thus, we can assume that this area was an ancient population center,

The Book of Mormon territory of western New York as laid out in the author's book, *The Lost Lands of the Book of Mormon.*

which this author believes was none other than the land of Zarahemla during the Nephite Era.

Artifacts of all types have been found in this region, including large skeletons. However, most of the burial mounds were nothing more than piles of bones which were covered with earth, much like the burial given those who died during the siege of Ammonihah in the Book of Mormon.

> Nevertheless, after many days their dead bodies were heaped up upon the face of the earth, and they were covered with a shallow covering. And now so great was the scent thereof that the people did not go in to possess the land of Ammonihah for many years. (Alma 16:11)

Not all burials can be attributed to warfare, however. Evidence that others were given a more thoughtful burial is evidenced by the discovery of bones found more carefully arranged, such as those found in Cattaraugus country (which is considered the more local land of Nephi in this author's *The Lost Lands of the Book of Mormon*).

> In making an excavation, eight skeletons, buried in a sitting posture and at regular intervals of space, so as to form a circle within the mound, were disinterred. Some slight appearance yet existed to show that framework had inclosed the dead at time of interment.
>
> These ontological remains were of very large size, but were so much decomposed that they mostly crumbled to dust. The relics of art here disclosed were also of a peculiar and interesting character—amulets, chisels, etc., of elaborate workmanship, resembling the Mexican and Peruvian antiquities.[4]

Such richly endowed burial sites provide invaluable information regarding the civilization that once occupied the region. However, as interesting as these burial sites were, of even greater interest to early explorers were the remnants of fortifications found scattered all across the countryside. Squier was of the opinion that, although they differed somewhat in certain particulars, the fortifications found in New York belonged to the same grand system as those of Ohio and the west generally. However, because evidence of Indian occupation in New York extends back so many centuries he concluded that if the earthen works in New York were of a remote age, then they were either built by the Iroquois, or some contemporary nation, or were secondarily occupied by them.[5] Now, this hypotheses was a very astute one, for when the Lamanites had completely exterminated the Nephites, they undoubtedly used their empty Nephite fortifications for their own purposes, since they continued to war amongst themselves throughout the ages. The scriptures tell us:

> The Lamanites are at war one with another; and the whole face of this land is one continual round of murder and bloodshed; and no one knoweth the end of the war. (Morm. 8:8)

We must remember that the Lamanites spent centuries trying to usurp this goodly territory from the Nephites, and, now that it was theirs, battle for tribal dominion undoubtedly began. Thus, warfare continued in the Cumorah lands even after the Nephites had been destroyed. The territory most likely changed hands many times over the centuries, for traces of aboriginal occupation in this region "is probably greater than any equal extent of territory north of the Floridas."[6]

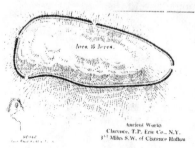

Ancient work, Livingston Co., New York. Squier, *Antiquities of the State of New York.*

This is not surprising, for not only did the Jaredites occupy this region for over a millennium and a half, and after them the Nephites, but the Lamanites continued to occupy it until the time of European contact.

~ ~ ~

Although the numerous fortifications found in New York are similar in certain respects to those found in Ohio, there are differences which are worthy of note. In *Pre-Historic Races,* Foster informs us, "The region adjacent to Lake Erie, comprehending Northern Ohio and Western New York contains ancient earthworks which differ somewhat from those of the Ohio Valley. There is the same combination of mound and enclosures, about which the ditch invariably is on the *outside* of the parapets."[7] However small this information may seem, it nonetheless places Moroni and the Nephites in western New York, for those fortifications found in New York resemble in every whit those built by Moroni, with ditches on the outside.

> Teancum, by the orders of Moroni, caused that they should commence laboring in digging a ditch round about the land, or the city, Bountiful.
>
> And he caused that they should build a breastwork of timbers upon the inner bank of the ditch; and they cast up dirt out of the ditch against the breastwork of timbers; and thus they did cause the Lamanites to labor until they had encircled the city of Bountiful round about with a strong wall of timbers and earth to an exceeding height. (Alma 53:3–4)

In Alma we gain even more insights to the way Moroni built his fortifications:

> And he caused that upon those works of timbers there should be a frame of pickets built upon the timbers round about; and they were strong and high.
>
> And he caused towers to be erected that overlooked those works of pickets, and he caused places of security to be built upon those towers, that the stones and the arrows of the Lamanites could not hurt them. (Alma 50:2–4)

MacLean noted such observatories and alarm posts in his various explorations. He also noted their signal stations and watch towers, for all were visible before white settlements obliterated them with the axe and plow. The similarities between those built by Moroni and those found in western New York can be found in the works of McIntosh as well. He records:

> These forts were generally speaking, erected on the most commanding ground. The walls or breastwork were earthen, The ditches were on the exterior of the works. . . . The trenches were in some cases deep and wide, and in other shallow and narrow; and the breastworks varied in altitude from three to eight feet. They sometimes had one and sometimes two entrances, as was to be inferred from there being no ditch at those places. When the works were protected by a deep ravine, or a stream of water, no ditch was to be seen. The areas of these forts varied from two to six acres; and the form was generally an irregular ellipse; and in some of them fragments of earthenware and pulverized substances, supposed to have been originally human bones were to be found.
>
> These fortifications, thus diffused over the interior of our country have been generally considered as surpassing the skill, patience and industry of the Indian race . . . and were lost in the abysses of unexplored antiquity.[8]

MacLean tells of an old legend, which has it "that the old forts had not been built by the Indians, but belonged to a long ago people, who were of white complexion, and skilled in the arts."[9]

Squire, who investigated so many of the earth works in New York, found the fortifications in the region were "too numerous to have been built for mere stations." Moreover, because human bones were found in them, he believed, instead, that they were used for war purposes. No one who ever explored the Cumorah lands of western New York before it was taken over by white settlements ever doubted that this region was the scene of ancient warfare.

Squire comments on the number of fortifications found:

> More than 1,000 sites in Ontario, Livingston, Genesee and Monroe Counties. Nearly 500 sites charted in Monroe County alone. In Genesee County are over 100 fortified

hilltops and strongholds, and similar number of burial sites, and nearly 50 true mounds. It thus appears that long before the coming of the white man, this region was settled by active and vigorous people. Their villages were along rivers, creeks, and lakes. Their camps upon the hills, their fortifications in strategic places difficult to assault. There is not an area of like size in the United States east of the Ohio and north of the Mason Dixon Line where evidences of aboriginal occupation are so abundant.[10]

It was not difficult to surmise the purposes for many of the earthen works found in the region. Some were towns, others villages, but, like the numerous fortifications in the area, each was fortified against enemy invasion. Squier estimates that at least two hundred fifty such fortifications filled the region. And that was just the number that survived the centuries.

Professor Turner was another who did not hesitate to declare that all the fortified hills in western New York had been erected by "a race which peopled this country before the Indians," and who had raised many monuments greatly exceeding the power of the Indians, and who lived at a remote era.[11] Josiah Priest concurred, and suggested further that the aborigines of America were the usurpers of this goodly region, who, "by force of bloody warfare exterminated the original inhabitants," and then "took possession of their country and property."[12]

Such assumptions were commonplace during the eighteenth and nineteenth centuries, for although Cyrus Thomas and others were totally convinced the ancestors of the Indians had built the mounds, far too much evidence existed that a superior race once occupied the region to disregard that notion altogether.

~ ~ ~

The uneasy sense that something terrible took place in this region many ages ago can still be felt by those who climb to the top of Cumorah or walk the surrounding territories. Words fail as one envisions that blood-splattered battlefield,

Michigan Relic. Note fortified building and
fort in lower right corner. Wayne May,
*Ancient American Magazine.*

and tears surface when one contemplates the loss of that once
great nation who, because of pride, forgot their Savior and
turned to wickedness. Relics of that terrible war are still being
discovered today. Unfortunately, so many were found during
the early years of colonization that many were simply dis-
posed of. No one truly understood the treasures they had in
their possession or the history behind those they so casually
acquired and then just as casually discarded. Numerous implements of warfare have been dug up in various places throughout the state, which provides undeniable evidence that terrible
wars were waged in the region throughout the ages— with
none greater than those fought by both the Nephite and Jaredite nations around the Hill Ramah/Cumorah at the end of their
respective eras.

How could anyone doubt this land was indeed populated
by those whose history is contained in the Book of Mormon,
for the story of their life and times can be read in the land.

There can be no doubt that warfare, blood, and horror rained down hard upon these regions.

~   ~   ~

Even so, in spite of such ghastly scenes as must have been conjured up in the minds of those who walked the battlefields around Cumorah, the entire region has always been lush and beautiful. The landscape is one of both flat plains and rolling hills and is simply filled with lakes, ponds, rivers, creeks, and cascading water-

Michigan Relic depicting two opposing armies. Note two figures at top, one in crown and one in feathered headdress. Wayne May, *Ancient American Magazine.*

falls. Forests filled with a great variety of trees and vegetation cover the entire landscape, and beautiful pastures fill the fertile plains and valleys. It is no wonder both the Nephites and Jaredites chose this place for their last stand, for the abundance of natural resources in the region were needed to sustain them during those years of gathering prior to their last and final battles. It would be difficult to dismiss the remarkable similarities between this bountiful region and the territory known only as "the land of many waters" in the scriptures. "No place on the American continent can so faithfully be called the land of many waters as the western half of New York state, and no other place in the hemisphere bears such evidence of having been an ancient battlefield."[13]

This fruitful land was filled with natural resources including those needed to produce weapons of war. In fact, this may be one reason this land was chosen by both the Nephites and Jaredites as a place of gathering and preparation before their final battles.

> Many ammunition plants have been found in western New York where ancient warriors fashioned their implements of war. The most famous one is called Flint Mine Hill, which is located in Greene County. In this hill was found a vein of flint one mile long and 900 feet wide. For centuries the ancient inhabitants have fashioned their flint points in that historic quarry. It was so well concealed by natural protection that it was not discovered until 1924.

> Enormous dumps of quarry refuse, twenty feet deep in places, marked the spot where they had worked the flint mine for generations. The area contained 'hundreds of train loads' of quarry refuse. All kinds of flint weapons were found in the cavity. The first scientist to examine the old munition factory found a vast supply of arrow points which were distributed among many private and public collections. In addition to the small point they found 3,000 hammer-stones after a few hours searching. . . . It has been examined by many scientists who have estimated that from 50 to 100 artisans worked there at a time over a period of more than 1,000 years. Some authorities estimate that the ruins found there represent an intermittent labor covering 5,000 years.

> Thousands of arrowheads, fine blades, hammer-stones, axes, large blades, and a variety of well-fashioned tools were found strewn over the area. Among the tons of specimens that were found on that historic hill were red slate, jasper felsite, argilite, white quartz, ryolite, and a high grade of compact light flint flecked with darker blotches. . . .

> The Museums in New York state are filled with the instruments of warfare that had been fashioned by the red man and so freely used in that historic area. The opinion is expressed in all those relic halls that western New York was

Stone weapons.
Squier and Davis, *Ancient Monuments,* 1848.

the site of an ancient battlefield. There is more evidence of a well planned defensive warfare in that locality than there is in any other region on the American Continent. It is the opinion of most scholars that the defenses on the drumlin hills were prepared by a people more civilized than the Indians and were exterminated by the inferior race who were still in possession of the country when Columbus discovered this land.[14]

Due to the untiring efforts of such men and Squier, Priest, Turner and others, we can almost visualize the sweeping hoards of Lamanites pressing down on the Nephites in their last stand at Cumorah. We can almost hear the cries of those whose fate was sealed and can almost see the terrible scene of destruction that spread out for miles as thousands upon thousands of Nephites perished on that bloody battlefield.

Who can doubt that this land was indeed populated by a "vanished race." The evidence of their demise is present everywhere. In fact, the evidence that battles of complete destruction took place around the Hill Cumorah is absolutely overwhelming. Yet rather than accept the Book of Mormon's account of such a people, far too many disregard that sacred text and look instead for more fantastic and exotic origins for those whose bones were found throughout the region. Consequently, the general public still wonders who these ancient inhabitants were, where they came from and why they so mysteriously disappeared. Even so, they almost universally acknowledge their superiority to the Indians.

The fanciful tales of the eighteenth and nineteenth centuries pale in comparison to the true story of the Mound Builders; a story circulated throughout the country shortly after the translation of the Book of Mormon. Unfortunately, few at that time could accept that historical record, for far too many theories about the origins of the Mound Builders had come and gone over the years, and this one seemed the most fantastic of all. And it was! Especially in light of the magnificent events that transpired at the appearance of the resurrected Savior among them, for it would be that visit and the out-pouring of the Spirit that would propel the entire eastern woodlands into an era of peace that lasted an unprecedented two hundred years. Thus, we also need to discover just how the limited lands of the Book of Mormon fit into the entire mound building region, for the events of that marvelous occasion undoubtedly affected the entire territory.

~ ~ ~

## Notes

1. Thomas, *12th Annual Report of the Bureau of Ethnology,* 525.
2. Ibid., 526.
3. Ibid., 528.
4. Ibid., 543.
5. Squier, *Antiquities of the State of New York,* 139.
6. Ibid., 35.
7. Foster, *Pre-Historic Races,* 144.
8. McGavin and Bean, *Geography of the Book of Mormon,* 78.
9. Ibid., 83.
10. Ibid., 65.
11. Turner, *Pioneer History of the Holland Purchase of Western New York,* 17–18.
12. Priest, *American Antiquities,* 331.
13. McGavin and Bean, *Geography of the Book of Mormon,* 26.
14. Ibid, 87–88.

Chapter Nine

# Piecing the Puzzle Together

In our continuing efforts to understand how the Nephite civilization equates with the ancient Mound Builders, we need to explore areas beyond the limited regions of Book of Mormon territory, for the mounds built up by that ancient people have been found throughout the entire eastern woodlands. How, then, do the Nephites and Lamanites of western New York fit into that over-all picture? In searching for answers to such questions, we must draw heavily upon the archeological findings of those in the last century, for prior to that time, far too much emphasis was placed on conjecture and suppositions born out of personal bias, often faulty or incomplete information, and sometimes even fraudulent discoveries. Therefore, we must bow to the findings of those in the Twentieth Century if we are to have any success at all in piecing together this complicated puzzle. While opinions still differ on certain points, most are now in complete agreement that three different mound building cultures were present in the woodlands at various points in history.

Although evidence of Jaredite occupation has been found in more archaic sites, the Mound Builders lived during the second mound building epoch. This era is known today as the "Woodland" or the "Adena-Hopewell period," which some suggest existed between 1000–500 B.C and A.D. 400-500. A third epoch, called the "Mississippian," took place between A.D. 700 and 1700.[1] The time period of greatest interest to our quest, however, will be the Woodland Epoch, for the remnants of that civilization still dot the eastern third of the country and give us by far the most information to consider. It also most closely matches the time attributed the Nephite era (600 B.C.–A.D. 400).

~ ~ ~

The greatest concentration of mounds from the Woodland Epoch have been along the Ohio, Sciota, Muskingum and the Miame Rivers in what is now Ohio State. This is a beautiful region with hills and grasslands spreading out across the land; a land filled with forests and an infinite variety of birds and wildlife. All who entered the region were amazed by its beauty, but even more amazed by the vast number of mounds found all across the landscape.

E. G. Squier comments:

> [In] the regions watered by the Ohio and its tributaries . . . we find numberless mounds. . . . These are by far the most imposing class of our aboriginal remains and impress utmost sensibly with the numbers and power of the people who built them. . . .The number of may be safely estimated at 10,000. . . . There are few sections of the country of equal extent which embraces so large a number of ancient works.

Excavation of the various mounds provided archeologists with a treasury of information regarding the civilization belonging to the Mound Builders. But, of particular interest, were the skulls found, for some were apparently long and narrow while others were broad or round. In an effort to understand such differences, the skulls of several ancient individuals were examined by Dr. Morton, an eminent craniologist, who declared the round skulls resembled the Toltecans. Nott and Gliddon later expanded that theory to include all Native American races.[2]

The story of the Mound Builders begins to materialize rather quickly at this point, for because of certain differences in their burial customs, artifacts, and ceremonial customs most authorities are in agreement that two distinct cultures existed in the region during the Woodland Epoch; the long-headed "Hopewells" from the north and the round-headed "Adenas" from the south. Thus, archeological evidence indicates that two separate cultures lived side by side during the Woodland Epoch, with each having similar cultural traits yet living essentially different lifestyles, just like the Nephites and Lamanites described in the Book of Mormon.

~ ~ ~

(Since Nott and Gliddon equate the round-headed Adena skulls with the Native American Indians, which the L.D.S. community will recognize as Lamanites, the two terms, Adena and Lamanite, will be used interchangeably in the following pages. Likewise, since the long-headed Hopewell are considered by all to be a superior race, they may represent the Nephites. Thus, the terms Hopewell and Nephite will be used interchangeably as well.)

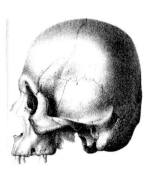

Skull from mound in Scioto Valley. Squier and Davis, *Ancient Monuments,* 1848.

~ ~ ~

Theories about the origin of the Mound Builders have literally filled volumes over the years, but once the Adena skulls found in so many mounds were equated with the Indians, there was no longer any hesitancy in attributing many of the mounds to the ancestors of the Native Americans. Thus, in some small way, the descendants of the Adena culture seem to have found their place in history, but from whence they came still seems to mystify the world.

The origin of the Hopewells, on the other hand, is still being debated, for there were no long-headed races on the continent when early explorers first came upon the scene. In spite of the on-going questions about their origins, however, it is now commonly believed their culture began in the north near the eastern end of Lake Ontario, which this author considers the heart of Book of Mormon territory. Don W. Dragoo, curator of the Carnegie Museum and author of *Mounds for the Dead,* informs us that the long-headed populations are best known in western, central, and northern New York State and lower Ontario. While similar cultures show up in Ohio, Michigan, Minnesota, and Indiana, Dragoo informs us that the long-headed populations were dominant in New York during that time period.

While many puzzled over the sudden appearance of these cultures in the woodlands. and wonder how the Adenas, so different from the Hopewells, came to dominate the Ohio Valley, while the Hopewells remained in those regions more to the north, the L.D.S. community will quickly recognize that the Adenas (Lamanites) were nothing more than off-shoots from the Hopewells (Nephites), but because of their hatred for one another they kept themselves as far apart as possible.

The story of that mutually agreed upon separation is found in the Book of Mormon and reveals that an irreconcilable family rift took place in the family of Lehi soon after their arrival in the promised land. Laman and Lemuel, the eldest sons of Lehi had always been contentious, but, because of their hatred for their younger brother, Nephi, they completely turned from the ways of the Lord and sought to take away his life. Now, after being led from sure destruction in Jerusalem to a land choice above all others, the Lord cursed them for their wickedness. Thus, they, and their posterity, subsequently became a dark and loathsome people, full of mischief and idleness.

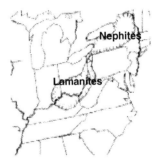

Nephite occupation in New York and Lamanite occupation in Ohio.

In consequence of such family rivalries and because Nephi and his followers feared for their lives, the Nephites, (those who followed Nephi) left the land of their first inheritance and moved further northward into western New York, while the Lamanites, (those who followed Laman) apparently followed the course of the Ohio River southward. Although their greater populations remained a respectable distant apart, the Lamanites were so determined to destroy the Nephites they eventually took over much of Nephite territory and set up societies of their own throughout the land of Nephi, forcing the Nephites further northward into Zarahemla.

Although Lamanites ultimately infiltrated Nephite territory, archeological evidence bears out the fact that the greater portion of their cultures remained separate from one another. One reason for such an assumption is given by MacLean in his *Mound Builders*:

> A map of the earth-works found in Ohio indicated three things. 1- that a belt of country running through central Ohio from east to west was entirely devoid of ancient earth-works, 2- that south of this belt were numerous military and religious enclosures, and 3- that north of this belt were numerous military works but no sacred enclosures.[3]

Because the soil in this central belt is fertile, MacLean questioned why there was no occupation in this central territory other than to conclude that those in the region fully intended to keep themselves separate from one another. He speculated further that "if the same nations had occupied both regions we would certainly meet with sacred enclosures."[4] He, therefore, concluded there must have been two distinct nations living in the land, each with different sympathies and, thus, placing themselves widely apart, just as the scriptures tell us the Nephites and Lamanites did. Without that scriptural account to rely on, however, Dragoo, simply speculated that the long-headed people were confined to the lands surrounding the Great Lakes because the round-headed Adenas had already staked their claim to the Ohio Valley.

Even so, as a result of such informed opinions, we have an archeological picture strikingly similar to the one described in the Book of Mormon, with the Nephites occupying the lands to the north and the Lamanites just to the south of them.

While the scriptural account of that drama is confined to the limited regions of southwestern New York, with the Nephites continually moving northward and then spreading eastward into the land of many waters, the more expanded archeological picture has the Nephites also spreading westward along the lower Great Lakes. In fact, Prufer, a noted researcher of the twentieth century, follows the journey of the long-headed Hopewells from western and central New York, westward as far as

Long-headed populations have been traced from New York westward as far as Michigan.

Michigan. Interestingly, Dragoo noticed several parallels between long-headed people in New York and other long-headed people in Illinois. Thus, it appears that at some point in time the Hopewell also migrated southward into Illinois.

~ ~ ~

Research also indicates the Hopewells were more enlightened than the Adena. This is another interesting parallel between the Nephite civilization and the Mound Builders, for the scriptures inform us that because of wickedness, the Lamanites were never permitted to reach the same heights of excellence as their more righteous Nephite brethren. Nonetheless, for reasons still unknown to the world in general, authorities such as Griffin believe the people from New York entered southern Ohio around 50 B.C. and A.D. 150, and, together with their round-headed brethren, spawned a culture so superior to anything before that time that it lasted for two hundred years. Thus, Dragoo calls Hopewell "the catalyst' that sparked the transformation and expansion that occurred in the Adena way of life." The period of time in which this combined culture thrived has since been named the Hopewellian Epoch. It was a magnificent time; a time similar in every way to the Nephite "golden age, "when both Nephites and Lamanites lived together in peace.

(Most charts which carry dates relevant to the advent of the Hopewellian Epoch show dates ranging from 200 B.C. to 50 B.C., with most straddling the middle at 100 B.C. While such dating methods are universally recognized as nothing more than suggested time frames, with as much as a plus or minus of one hundred to three hundred years, most reflect a definite rise in culture around the time of Christ which lasted about two hundred years before beginning its decline and then completely disappearing around A.D. 400.)

Without the scriptural account of those events that took place around the time of the Savior, it has been difficult for the archeological world to explain the rapid change in cultural habits which culminated in the birth of the Hopewellian culture. Nonetheless, Web and Snow expressed the opinion that "the mixing and blending of two different peoples at this time brought about a hybrid vigor, genetically and culturally, that resulted in the magnificence of Ohio Hopewell"[5] Dragoo comments:

> The transformation was not gradual but quite abrupt. . . . However, stratigraphic and topological evidence does exist for an alteration of Adena Culture that cannot be adequately explained on the basis of internal evolution alone. Since these changes in Late Adena were links to Hopewell, it would seem not only possible but also probably that the Lenid {long- headed} peoples of Hopewell were the catalyst in this transformation either by direct physical participation or as a potent external stimulus, or both.[6]

In searching for answers to this sudden rise in culture at this particular point in time, we must turn to the scriptures and discover just what was happening in the region prior to the Savior's birth. Only by doing so will we discover just why there was such a dramatic change in both cultures shortly before the birth of Christ and why it lasted for such a long time.

While many are still puzzled by the matter, students of the Book of Mormon will remember that just prior to the time of Christ there was a great conversion among the Lamanites. Warfare had been raging back and forth between the Nephites and Lamanites since they first entered the promised land nearly six hundred years earlier. And this, because the Lamanites were totally convinced the Nephites had wronged their first parents by usurping authority from them and by taking their sacred records which they felt rightly belonged to them. Thus, they were determined to either wipe the Nephites off the face of the earth or place them in subjection. Consequently, only short periods of peace had ever been enjoyed by either people. Warfare dominated the scene continuously from their entrance into the promised land to just before the birth of the Savior. In fact, the Lamanites had become so aggressive in their determination to destroy the Nephites they had actually succeeded in taking over a large portion of their territory by this time.

During those turbulent years, Nephi, the son of Helaman, became so weary of the wickedness of his people, supposing they would lose all their lands to the Lamanites if they did not repent, gave up the judgment seat, and he, and his brother Lehi, went out among the people to preach the gospel. So filled were they with the power of God that a great many were converted and returned to the fold. Such power of persuasion was given them that eight thousand Lamanites who were also in Zarahemla entered the waters of baptism.

Armed with this success, Nephi and Lehi then departed into Lamanite territory in hopes they might convert those in the land of Nephi as well. Unfortunately, this desire was met with disappointment, for the Lamanites immediately threw them into prison and were about to destroy them. But, thankfully, the Lord had other plans.

The Savior had always been mindful of his Lamanite children. He was perfectly aware that, although they constantly warred with their Nephite brethren, they were only living those laws that had been handed down by their fathers. He also understood that even though their war-like natures surfaced during their altercations with the Nephites, they were friendly to one another and experienced lasting bonds of love between husbands and wives and parents and children. Because of these various circumstances, and because of their inclination to remain steadfast once enlightened, the Lord was lenient with them. Thus, when Lehi and Nephi entered their land for the express purpose of preaching the gospel, the Lord was prepared to to do a marvelous work among the Lamanites. Yea, a marvelous work and a wonder, for the time was soon at hand when he would be in their midst and would minister to them.

When the Lamanites stretched forth their hands to slay Nephi and Lehi, the walls of the prison began to shake. The frightened Lamanites looked and beheld, to their surprise, that their captives were encircled by fire, yet were not burned. Then, within moments, a dark cloud overshadowed them and out of the darkness a voice was heard: "Repent ye, repent ye, and seek no more to destroy my servants whom I have sent unto you to declare good tidings" (Hel. 5:29).

Again the earth shook, and again the same message was heard, and still the cloud engulfed them. Then, after falling to their knees in repentance and crying out for forgiveness, the cloud lifted, the veil parted, and a glorious spiritual manifestation fell upon the scene. Within moments the Lamanites, too, were encircled by fire, and "the heavens opened and angels came down out of heaven and ministered to them" (Hel. 5:48).

What a glorious experience that must have been. Words alone could not have expressed the grandeur of that soul changing occurrence. So powerful was that experience, that much of the Lamanite nation was changed profoundly from that time forth.

About three hundred Lamanites witnessed that wondrous manifestation. So great was their conversion that when the scene finally closed they immediately "went forth" and began to preach to their brethren.

All this transpired just twenty-nine years before the birth of the Savior and may well have marked the birth of the Hopewellian Epoch, for, at long last, the Nephites and Lamanites walked together as brothers.

Archeological evidence bears this out as well, for there is evidence that trade relations were at an all time high at this point in history. We learn of that time from Helaman:

> And behold, there was peace in all the land, insomuch that the Nephites did go into whatsoever part of the land they would, whether among the Nephites or the Lamanites.
>
> And it came to pass that the Lamanites did also go whithersoever they would, whether it were among the Lamanites or among the Nephites; and thus they did have free intercourse one with another, to buy and to sell, and to get gain, according to their desire.
>
> And it came to pass that they became exceedingly rich, both the Lamanites and the Nephites; and they did

have an exceeding plenty of gold, and of silver, and of all manner of precious metals, both in the land south and in the land north. . . .

And behold, there was all manner of gold in both these lands, and of silver, and of precious ore of every kind; and there were also curious workmen, who did work all kinds of ore and did refine it; and thus they did become rich.

They did raise grain in abundance, both in the north and in the south; and they did flourish exceedingly, both in the north and in the south. And they did multiply and wax exceedingly strong in the land. And they did raise many flocks and herds, yea, many fatlings.

Behold their women did toil and spin, and did make all manner of cloth, of fine-twined linen and cloth of every kind, to clothe their nakedness. And thus the sixty and fourth year did pass away in peace. (Hel. 6:7–9, 11–13)

Not only did peace prevail in the land, but apparently "an elaborate exchange network of nearly continental proportions emerged, capable of amassing resources from the Rocky Mountains to the Appalachians and from the Great Lakes to the Gulf of Mexico."[7] Evidence of this is born out by the fact that precious trade goods from all regions have been found in the mounds.

Mound sites throughout the region have yielded large quantities of the same highly valued items: tens of thousands of freshwater pearls from the Mississippi and its tributaries; Great Lakes copper . . . hammered into ear spools, pan pipes, breast plates, and various decorative forms; silver from Ontario; hematite from Michigan; chert from Illinois; Upper Mississippi Valley galena for white paint and sparkling powder, . . . ceramic figurines from Illinois, Ohio, and Wisconsin; . . . flint blades and carved soapstone pipes from Ohio; mica from southern Appalachia (which was often separated into thin sheets and cut into artfully shaped human hands, birds, and snakes); crystalline quartz from Arkansas; obsidian, chalcedony, and bear's teeth from the Rocky Mountains; shell beads and whole marine shells, shark's teeth, alligator teeth, barracuda jaws, and turtle shells from the Gulf of Mexico; and Gulf Coast stamped pottery.[8]

Without question, there was an era of excellence in the eastern portion of the United States just prior to, and for a period of two hundred years following, the time of Christ. We must be reminded, however, that the history contained in the scriptures is of the limited regions of western New York. Therefore the peaceful interaction described in the scriptures speaks only of those who lived in that region. All of western New York, both northward and southward, were involved in this new interactive phase. But, whether this time of peace extended beyond the Cumorah lands to those regions "round about" the scriptures do not address. By turning to archeological evidence, however, we can clearly see that something big was happening in the Ohio Valley at this very point in history.

Obviously, the entire region was filled with people, not just the small territory occupied by those whose history is contained in Book of Mormon. Therefore, we might speculate about whether this mass conversion of the Lamanites included those in Ohio. Although, the scriptures do not say, reason would tell us that since the Lamanites were preaching throughout both the lands northward and southward of Book of Mormon territory (see Hel. 6:4–6), it would seem likely they were also preaching to their brethren in Ohio, for it was the land of their first inheritance. If this be true, then it would seem the newly converted Lamanites, in union with their righteous Nephite brethren, did indeed influence the Lamanite societies in surrounding regions for the better, even to the over-turning of their inclinations toward false worship and instructing them in the Law of Moses.

> And I would that ye should behold that the more part of them [Lamanites] are in the path of their duty, and they do walk circumspectly before God, and they do observe to keep his commandments and his statutes and his judgements according to the law of Moses. (Hel. 15: 5)

If, as suggested, the missionary efforts of the Lamanites extended southward into regions along the Ohio River, and

Marietta Works in Ohio.
Squier and Davis, *Ancient Monuments,* 1848.

supposing their brethren were receptive to their preaching, there
is reason to suggest that the grand earthen enclosures built up
during the Hopewellian era may well have been sacred in
nature. According to the old Indian Prophet De-coo-dah, it was
within the walls of such enclosures that many of their younger
prophets were taught and instructed in matters of religion. In
fact, it may well be that those magnificent works were actually
Lamanite temples, built up for the purpose of worshiping Jehovah and officiating in the Law of Moses. If this be the case,
then at least some of the sacrificial altars found in the region
would have been used to officiate in the Law of Moses, with
its attendant animal sacrifices, rather than the perverted sacrificial rites that may well have been their common custom before
their conversion. (Blood sacrifice would have been done away
with, however, after the Savior's visit among them.)

~ ~ ~

As conversions increased, the fear of traveling through
Lamanite territory decreased. Thus, while the greater number

of Nephites remained nestled away in Zarahemla, it appears, because of the number of Hopewell skulls found in Ohio, which date to this very time period, that some at least, were also migrating southward into Lamanite territory during this interactive phase.

Evidence suggests that Hopewell from the west were also migrating into Ohio at this point in history, which has led some to question whether the movement of Hopewell into Ohio came predominantly from New York, or perhaps from the long-headed populations in Illinois, which by this time had produced a rather large population. Prufer, a noted authority on the subject, believes the starting point was probably Ontario or Central New York.

> The work of Olaf Prufer and his colleagues produces a picture of the long-headed Hopewells moving out of the Northeast into Illinois and then into Ohio, picking up useful traits as they went and creating in Ohio a dynamic cultural center whose influence radiated outward over a wide area. The starting point of this movement may have been in Ontario and central New York State.[9]

Even so, because of the number of similar artifacts found in both Illinois and Ohio, some still suggest that the Hopewell in Illinois may have had more interaction with Ohio Hopewell than those from New York. Even Dragoo recognized that "the New York populations did not share the same fruits of the Ohio Hopewell as their western cousins did." Nevertheless, Dragoo believed "the similarities shared by the

The spread of New York and Illinois Hopewell into Ohio during the golden era.

Hopewell in Ohio, Illinois, and New York were neither accidental, nor merely the result of trade, but the result of a common physical and cultural heritage."[10] Dragoo believed the
presence of Hopewellian materials and sites in the central
Ohio Valley seemed to indicate that the Hopewells drove a
"wedge into Adena territory" from both the north and the west.
Because of this influx from both directions, the long-headed
populations eventually came to dominating the Ohio Valley.

~ ~ ~

Vault burial.
Thomas, *12th Annual Report of Bureau of Ethnology.*

A great many changes took place during the Hopewellian
age. The Adena began the construction of elaborate log tombs
instead of the simpler burial pits of Early Adena. Such tombs
were constructed inside a type of burial house which was then
covered over until earth enclosed the entire structure. Dragoo
informs us that fine artifacts were interred with each individual buried in these sub-floor tombs or log enclosures, rather
than the earlier practice of placing the artifacts with many
individuals scattered throughout the mounds. The Hopewell,
too, used burial tombs, but, unlike the Adena, they interred
their dead in stone cists set into pits, or under plain ground (i.e.
not under mounds). As time passed, the old Adena practice of
cremation nearly completely disappeared, and they, too, began
to inter their dead in stone cists, or under plain ground.
Undoubtedly due to Hopewell influence.

Their artistry took on new dimensions as well, and a new
wave of building began. Shaffer informs us:

133

The Hopewell carried Adena proficiencies to new heights. They fashioned metal and stone into ornaments of surpassing beauty. In contrast to the simple circular embankments that sometimes enclosed Adena burial mounds, they created increasingly grander ceremonial compounds in the form of marvelously varied and mathematically precise geometrical shapes, plazas, and avenues that sometimes extended for miles.[11]

The mound building region ultimately became a region of wonderfully built ceremonial centers "dominated by commerce and shared ideas." The hub of this ancient empire was

Circular compound. Nadaillac, *Pre-Historic America.*

located in Ohio, which spread out from there in various directions. Consequently, the once Adena held lands ultimately became a territory of mixed cultures during the Hopewellian era, with the Hopewell far the superior.

Even the funeral articles placed in the mounds differed between early Adena and the later Hopewellian Epoch. Silverberg describes those differences for us. (While this combined empire is often referred to as the "Hopewellian Epoch," often those Hopewell who made such an impact on the Adena culture in Ohio are simply referred to as Ohio Hopewell.)

There is a stunning vigor about Ohio Hopewell. By comparison, the grave deposits of the Adena folk look sparse and poor. Hopewell displays a love of excess that shows itself—not only in the intricate geometrical enclosures and in the massive mounds, but in the gaudy displays in the tombs. To wrap a corpse from head to foot in pearls, to weight it down in many pounds of copper, to surround it with masterpieces of sculpture and pottery, and then to bury everything under tons of earth—this is the kind of wastefulness that only an amazingly energetic culture would indulge in.[12]

Apparently, an extravagance unknown before that time entered the region and was shared by people throughout the territory.

> From their heartland in southern Ohio, the Hopewell, by trade and travel, acquired and exchanged ideas over much of the continent east of the Great Plains. Hopewellian societies, however, did not constitute a political empire, but rather, as Joseph R. Caldwell of the Illinois State Museum once put it, an "interaction sphere"—a dominion of commerce and shared ideas.[13]

~ ~ ~

It is important to realize that even though the Hopewells influenced the budding Hopewellian era tremendously, the mound centers that flourished in Ohio and neighboring regions were built upon original Adena customs. The great mound centers originally built and maintained by the Adenas over the centuries simply became grander as the Hopewells entered their region. Dragoo informs us that "although the influence of the Hopewell on the Adena is most readily apparent in the artifacts, the most potent influence of all probably was the category of social organization," or, as Olaf Prufer put it, "Hopewellian elements are simply something added to and, to a limited extent, integrated with pre-existing local cultures." He comments further that, "Ohio Hopewell minus the elaborate ceremonial and artifactual trappings would not be much different from Adena." Such theories were based on comments by Webb and Snow who found among many late Adena sites, "the beginnings of many of the customs which in Hopewell blossomed into important and highly specialized traits."

~ ~ ~

The important changes that took place during this exceptional time was largely due to the new religious fervor of the Lamanites. However distorted, religion had always been an integral part of their culture, but once converted to the gospel of Jesus Christ, they experienced a religious zeal unknown before that time. In fact, so strong was their faith and so righteous had they become, that thirteen years from the time the sign was given of the Savior's birth, the more righteous Lamanites lost their curse and became a white and delightsome people again (see 3 Ne. 2:15).

This abrupt change in their physical appearance may also account for what appears to the archeological world to be a sudden influx of Hopewell into the Ohio Valley during the Hopewellian era, for once the curse was lifted, and supposing there was intermarriage with the Hopewell, the Adena would eventually have taken on many Long-headed characteristics. Prior to that time, any and all who mixed with the Lamanites were destined to take upon themselves the same curse as the Lamanites.

> And the skins of the Lamanites were dark, according to the mark which was set upon their fathers, which was a curse upon them because of their transgression and their rebellion against their brethren, who consisted of Nephi, Jacob, and Joseph, and Sam, who were just and holy men. . . .
>
> And it came to pass that whosoever did mingle his seed with that of the Lamanites did bring the same curse upon his seed. (Alma 3:6, 9)

With those dominant genes no longer in play, the Adena could now take on the traits of the Hopewell. Thus, rather than assign all the Hopewell skulls found in the region, which date to this period in time, to those who migrated in from other regions, the increase may have been due, in part, to the fact that many of the Adena had simply become Hopewell over the years. Dragoo confirms this supposition in the following comment.

The evidence from physical anthropological studies indicates that some "Adena like" individuals became, "to all intent and purposes," Hopewell people whether by a mingling of blood or by actual mixing of peoples.[14]

While there is every indication that Hopewells from both the north and west entered the Ohio Valley during the Hopewellian era, it may well be that, at least, some of the long- headed skulls found in Ohio belonged to the righteous Lamanites who had lost their curse.

This may also explain why the great ceremonial centers, which have been attributed to the Hopewell in Ohio, flourished during this interactive phase while such earthen monuments do not show up in New York. We must be reminded that this was a Lamanite custom, and even though their appearance and physiology may have changed after they proved themselves worthy, centuries of cultural conditioning may not have. Consequently, their mound building practices would have continued. They simply became grander and larger during the Hopewellian Epoch. Therefore, many of the mound centers in Ohio, which have been attributed to the Hopewell culture, may have been built by those Lamanites who had lost their curse and ultimately became Hopewell over the years. (We would assume they were now built up to worship the Savior instead of any former deities, however.)

While the scriptures tell us that many of the more righteous Lamanites enjoyed a rather dramatic physical change after their conversion, apparently not all of them enjoyed that experience, for archeological evidence indicates that at least twenty five percent of the populations in Ohio remained round-headed. In fact, as the long-headed people (whether Nephites or white Lamanites) began to dominate the Ohio Valley, archeological evidence indicates the round-headed Lamanites began to migrate westward and eventually came to dominate Illinois. Thus, we can see that the woodlands ultimately became a region of mixed cultures who traveled freely between lands and enjoyed a time of peaceful interaction.

~ ~ ~

Although many favorable changes took place in the woodlands during the years surrounding the birth of the Savior, the Gadianton Robbers were still a major plague to both the Nephites and Lamanites during the early years of the Hopewellian era and threatened their peaceful way of life. Unfortunately, far too many Nephites had already fallen under their spell and wickedness began to infiltrate every portion of the land. But, in fulfillment of prophecy, this ungodly band, along with the greater portion of the wicked, were ultimately destroyed when the great upheavals of nature that accompanied the Savior's crucifixion fell upon the region and swept them all away. Only the more righteous among them remained.

The death of the Savior marked a new episode in history for the Nephites and Lamanites, for at long last the wicked among both people had been dispatched home to their maker and the land was now cleansed of its idolatry. Of greater importance, however, is that the Savior himself was about to show himself to those faithful few who survived.

As might be expected, when the risen Lord ultimately appeared to his little flock in Bountiful, the outpouring of love was felt so profoundly by both the Nephites and Lamanites that the entire region was propelled into a golden age that lasted an unprecedented two hundred years. So great was their devotion to their Redeemer and so committed to his message of love and peace, that all lived as equals in a Zion oriented society, and never were they happier.

The mere fact they lived in continual peace for two hundred years is strong presumptive evidence that the entire region was involved in this golden era, for had those in outlying regions continued in their wicked state, they surely would have created mischief for the people of God, and would have tried to usurp power over them as they had done so consistently in the past. Apparently only the more righteous remained to enjoy that time of peace.

~ ~ ~

The magnificent Hopewellian Culture thrived for two hundred years before beginning its decline. Prufer believed the Hopewell went through a long and slow degeneration which may have lasted from two hundred to five hundred years, ending, perhaps, about A.D. 450. (Surprisingly close to the dates attributed to the decline and disappearance of the Nephite civilization, which gives added support to the premise that the Hopewells and the Nephites were one and the same.)

Prufer informs us that while the people in Illinois appear to have gradually declined sometime after A.D. 400, (which mixture of peoples, by this time, were predominantly Lamanites), the Hopewellian culture in New York "disappeared as suddenly as it did in Ohio,"[15]. This information reconciles perfectly with the scriptures, for the entire Nephite civilization had been gathered out from every land at this point in time and were all destroyed at Cumorah. Thus, those Hopewell from both Ohio and New York would have been destroyed at the same time.

Unfortunately, we have only a very brief historical record of what transpired in the eastern woodland during ancient times, for the Book of Mormon contains the history of only a limited region. We must remember travel was more difficult in ancient times, and journeying from one area to another was very difficult and time consuming. Therefore, "many" were called upon to record the happenings in their various territories. "And I shall also speak unto all nations of the earth and they shall write it" (2 Ne. 29:12).

We can feel confident that the histories of even those who lived in regions far beyond the bounds of Book of Mormon territory have been recorded and will one day come forth—in spite of men's total disregard for those numerous ancient tablets that have already been found and simply regarded as fakes or, even worse, destroyed. In the Lord's good time all knowledge will come forth. Thus, the efforts of the academic world to keep any knowledge of a people intelligent enough to have kept written records from surfacing in their own vain attempts to prove North America had not been inhabited by outsiders prior to Columbus will once and for all be spoiled. Until that time, however, we must do the best we can with reason, the scriptures, and the evidence provided by archeological research, to provide the answers we seek in reconciling the correlation between the Mound Builders and the people of the Book of Mormon.

The mounds in Ohio are magnificent and speak of a great time in history. Unfortunately, the history of those regions will only be revealed when their records are restored. What a story they will tell when they ultimately come forth. What a grand story, yet one for a future time!

~ ~ ~

## Zelph

By way of interest, there is an account of the excavation of the remains of a "white Lamanite" during the Prophet Joseph Smith's journey to Zion's Camp. Apparently they found the remains of an ancient warrior atop a large mound in Illinois. Seven men who witnessed the excavation wrote of this account. Although each had a different interpretation of those events, as might be expected, all agreed on the more important facts pertinent to that discovery. Reuben McBride's account is the shortest and the most succinct, covering the most important information which seemed to correspond nicely with all other accounts.

> Tuesday, [June] 3 [1834] visited the mounds. A skeleton was dug up [by] Joseph, said his name was Zelph a great warrior under the Prophet Onandagus. An arrow was found in his rib.[16]

Other accounts indicated he was a "white Lamanite" who was known from the Hill Cumorah, or eastern sea, to the Rocky Mountains, and that he died in battle.

The day following, on the banks of the Mississippi River, the Prophet wrote the following in a letter to Emma, his wife.

> The whole of our journey, in the midst of so large a company of social honest and sincere men, wandering over the Plaines of the Nephites, recounting occasionally the history of the Book of Mormon, roving over the mounds of that once beloved people of the Lord, picking up their skulls, and their bones, as a proof of its divine authenticity, and gazing upon a country and the fertility, the splendour and the goodness so indescribably, all serves to pass away time unnoticed.[17]

We might note here that Joseph readily recognized the surrounding countryside had once been Nephite territory. Of special interest to this account, however, is that those who were present when Zelph was excavated, said the Prophet proclaimed him to be a "white Lamanite."

Kenneth W. Godfrey, in his account of the controversy surrounding the various versions of the Zelph excavation, felt the time attributed the mounds in which these remains were found was "between perhaps 100 B.C. and A.D. 500," for artifacts from other mounds in the region dated to that very time period.[18] This means he must have lived during the Hopewellian Epoch, for the curse was taken from the more righteous Lamanites just thirteen years after the sign was given of the Savior's birth.

~ ~ ~

## Notes

1. Shaffer, *Native Americans before 1492*, 5.
2. MacLean, *Mound Builders*, 142.

3. MacLean, *Mound Builders,* 140.

4. Ibid.

5. Silverberg, *Mound Builders,* 200.

6. Dragoo, "Development of Adena Culture," 26.

7. Shaffer, *Native Americans before 1492*, 44.

8. Ibid.

9. Silverberg, *Mound Builders,* 223.

10. Dragoo, "Development of Adena Culture," 19.

11. *Mound Builders and Cliff Dwellers,* 25

12. Silverberg, *Mound Builders,* 219.

13. *Mound Builders and Cliff Dwellers,* 25

14. Dragoo, "Development of Adena Culture," 13.

15. Prufer, "Hopewell Complex," 64–66.

16. Godfrey, "Zelph Story," 34.

17. Jessee, *Personal Writings of Joseph Smith,* 324.

18. Godfrey, "Zelph Story," 47.

Chapter Ten

# His Other Sheep

Archeological evidence indicates the Hopewellian Epoch was a time of peaceful interaction between both the Adena and the Hopewell cultures. Not surprisingly, the scriptural account of the Nephites golden age took place at precisely the same time in history; a time when both the Nephites and Lamanites walked together as brothers. Although that era of peace appears to have begun shortly before the birth of the Christ, it reached its greatest heights after the Savior's visit following his death and resurrection. The Spirit was so strong during that sacred occasion that the hearts of men were changed profoundly and peace was established which lasted an unprecedented two hundred years. The Nephites and Lamanites had been warring with each other since they first entered the promised land six hundred years earlier. Therefore, we would have to assume this golden age of excellence was due solely to the impact of Christ's visit to the area, for only their great love for him could have caused such a disruption in their natural inclinations toward war and vengeance.

Although the scriptures detail that wonderful time in history, we might reasonably ask if this change in the hearts of otherwise war-like individuals extended beyond the bounds of Book of Mormon territory, for the Hopewellian Epoch was blossoming throughout the eastern woodlands. That it did so is substantiated by the scriptures, for they inform us the Lord visited others of his scattered flock after his visit to Bountiful. We can assume, therefore, that those he subsequently visited were changed as profoundly as the Nephites were, and that peace was established in those regions as well. Archeological evidence bears this out, for there is every indication that a period of peaceful interaction existed throughout the woodlands between 50 B.C. and A.D. 200.

Unfortunately, the scriptures are silent on the Lord's visit to other regions. The only source we have for information regarding such visitations comes to us from oral traditions handed down by various aboriginal tribes over the centuries. Some come from oral histories, others from long poetic chants used by some tribes to keep their histories alive. Still others from the stories told various early American writers who walked and talked with tribes all over the hemisphere. Such oral traditions were considered so important to most native races that they were carefully taught each succeeding generation in an effort to keep them from fading from memory. Although many became distorted over the years, early explorers were amazed by the numbers which spoke of a great white God who walked among them in more ancient times, and who taught them a higher law. Even more amazing were the similarities they found in the legends of tribes that were hundreds and even thousands of miles apart. Those from both North and South America speak of a bearded white man with strange marks in his hands who healed the sick and calmed the seas. He was said to have organized the priesthood wherever he went and did away with blood sacrifice, for the ultimate sacrifice had already been paid.

~ ~ ~

While such legends follow a path from the southern tip of South America through Canada in North America, nowhere else do we hear of an account as magnificent as the one described in the Book of Mormon. The Savior's appearance to his faithful flock in Bountiful was so glorious that words alone could not express the grandeur of that occasion. And this, because those who survived the destruction, which took place at the time of his crucifixion were those who had remained righteous in spite of the wickedness that had swept across the land. Those few righteous souls were actually privileged to hear the Father announce his Son: "Behold my Beloved Son, in whom I have glorified my name—hear ye him" (3 Ne. 11:7).

The stunned crowd watched as the Savior slowly descended and stood in their midst. Then, after complying with his directive to step forward and feel the wounds in his hands and feet, they fell to the ground and worshiped him. Only then did the Savior announce his Godhood.

> Behold, I am Jesus Christ, whom the prophets testified shall come into the world.
>
> And behold, I am the light and the life of the world; and I have drunk out of that bitter cup which the Father hath given me, and have glorified the Father in taking upon me the sins of the world, in the which I have suffered the will of the Father in all things from the beginning. (3 Ne. 11:10–11)

The Lord then taught them, and blessed them, and organized his church among them.

> And after this manner do they bear record: The eye hath never seen, neither hath the ear heard, before, so great and marvelous things as we saw and heard Jesus speak unto the Father;
>
> And no tongue can speak, neither can there be written by any man, neither can the hearts of men conceive so great and marvelous things as we both saw and heard Jesus

speak; and no one can conceive of the joy which filled our souls at the time we heard him pray for us unto the Father. . . .

And they arose from the earth, and he said unto them: Blessed are ye because of your faith. And now behold, my joy is full.

And when he had said these words, he wept, and the multitude bare record of it, and he took their little children, one by one, and blessed them, and prayed unto the Father for them.

And when he had done this he wept again. (3 Ne. 17:16–17, 20–22)

So much love permeated the scene that angels descended from Heaven and ministered to their children.

And he spake unto the multitude, and said unto them: Behold your little ones.

And as they looked to behold they cast their eyes towards heaven, and they saw the heavens open, and they saw angels descending out of heaven as it were in the midst of fire; and they came down and encircled those little ones about, and they were encircled about with fire; and the angels did minister unto them.

And the multitude did see and hear and bear record; and they know that their record is true for they all of them did see and hear, every man for himself; and they were in number about two thousand and five hundred souls; and they did consist of men, women, and children. (3 Ne. 17:23–25)

Nowhere else in the Americas do we hear of such an outpouring of the Spirit as was experienced by his faithful followers in Bountiful. Nonetheless, because of his great love for his entire flock, the Lord appeared to many of his sheep throughout the hemisphere—those who, although in their fallen state, were still more righteous than those who had been destroyed just prior to his coming.

> And verily verily, I say unto you that I have other sheep, which are not of this land, neither of the land of Jerusalem, neither in any parts of that land round about whither I have been to minister.
>
> For they of whom I speak are they who have not as yet heard my voice; neither have I at any time manifested myself unto them.
>
> But I have received a commandment of the Father that I shall go unto them, and that they shall hear my voice, and shall be numbered among my sheep, that there may be one fold and one shepherd; therefore I go to show myself unto them. (3 Ne. 16:1–3)

Thus, his journey to touch the lives of the scattered of Israel began. The next question that might be ask, however, is who were these other sheep? In speaking of the time following Savior's death and resurrection, the book of Mormon informs us: "The Lord God surely shall visit all the house of Israel at that day" (1 Ne. 19:11). We must assume, therefore that those he subsequently visited were a part of that illustrious family.

> But now I go unto the Father, and also to show myself unto the lost tribes of Israel, for they are not lost unto the Father, for he knoweth whither he hath taken them. (3 Ne. 17:4)

The Lord intended to visit "all" those of Israel who had been lost and scattered throughout the centuries. The very fact the Lord's mission was among the lost of Israel and not as yet among the Gentiles is found in 3 Nephi. In speaking of the Jews in Jerusalem, the Savior said:

> And verily, I say unto you again that the other tribes hath the Father separated from them; and it is because of their iniquity that they know not of them.
>
> And verily I say unto you, that ye are they of whom I said: Other sheep I have which are not of this fold; them also I must bring, and they shall hear my voice; and there shall be one fold, and one shepherd.

> And they understood me not, for they supposed it had been the Gentiles; for they understood not that the Gentiles should be converted through their preaching.
>
> And they understood me not that I said they shall hear my voice; and they understood me not that the Gentiles should not at any time hear my voice—that I should not manifest myself unto them save it were by the Holy Ghost.
>
> But behold, ye have both heard my voice, and seen me; and ye are my sheep, and ye are numbered among those whom the Father hath given me. (3 Ne. 15:20–24)

From this we learn that while the Savior would minister personally among the scattered of Israel, it would be through the powerful manifestation of the Holy Ghost that the Gentile nations would be converted. Thus, those legends which have filtered down to us over the years of a Pale God's visit to various aboriginal Americans may well have been the Savior's visit to his lost and scattered sheep, for the scriptures clearly indicate the Lamanites were a part of Israel.

~ ~ ~

From the various legends recounted by old Indian prophets, we learn that the Pale God's ministry in the New World caused quite a stir among the people. They heard of him long before he entered their territory, for news of his coming spread rapidly as he journeyed from region to region teaching, blessing, and organizing his church among each village and town he came to.

Because the means of travel and communication were so primitive in ancient times, twelve disciples were ordained in many regions so that each territory might have a priesthood hierarchy. Legends of such ordinations have been found in Georgia, Oklahoma, Washington, Oregon, California, and Mexico, with some legends simply stating that everywhere he stopped to teach "He trained twelve disciples, and one to be their leader who would accede to His title after He had gone."[1]

Each legend tells of a man with grey-green eyes wearing a white toga and golden sandals who traveled from city to city teaching the people about their Eternal Father. He changed their temple rites, healed the sick, raised the dead, and at times was seen to walk on water. He was welcomed and revered by all, and his fame and benevolent nature were spread throughout the land.

We cannot say specifically that this was the Savior, for other of his disciples, both in the Old World and the New were given great priesthood powers and were charged with the task of going throughout the world to preach the gospel. But, because of the strange marks in the Pale God's hands and his promise to return one day, many suggest it may well have been the Savior who, by the decree of his Father, was showing himself to his "other sheep."

This Prophet was known by many names. To the Polynesians he was the God, Wakea, while in Middle and South America, he was known as the Feathered Serpent. To the Mayas he was Kukulcan and to the Aztecs, Queszalcoatl. The Incas knew him as Kon-Tiki-Viracocha. In North America he was referred to as West Star Man, Waicoman, the Fair God who ruled the ocean, Peace Maker, Pale One, Dawn Star, Son of Creator, etc. He was known by others as Waikano, or Tacoma, as well as Ee-me-shee, the wind God. Others expanded that title and referred to him as the God of Wind and Water, for he was known to have calmed many great storms. He was known as Chee-Zoos, God of the Dawn Light, the Sacred One or sometimes simply as The Healer. Each region had their own version of his title and tales of his visit among them. Thus, as he moved through region after region, his fame spread, his gospel of love was embraced, and his memory forever retained in the histories of each tribe.

~ ~ ~

Fortunately, legends of this cultural hero's visit to North America have been preserved by various writers over the years. From Hansen's impressive collection, we learn that the Chippewa remember well the Pale God, as do the Algonquin of the eastern seaboard, who refer to him as "Chee-Zoos, God of the Dawn Light."[6] Legends gathered from Michigan reveal the Pale God organized their churches, changed their temple rites, gave them the Priesthood, and "taught them a secret language with certain signs of greeting."[7] It is said he told the ancient Puans that he came from across the great waters and spoke of his childhood, explaining that he was born of a virgin on a night when a bright star appeared in the sky.[8]

The great Algonquin Nation also has legends of the God of the Dawn Light's visit among them. They recount that "Machabo," as many call him, came to earth to bring them wisdom and to teach them a higher way. They further believe that when he returns he will bring them a golden age of peace.[2]

The Iroquois, who occupy much of Book of Mormon territory around New York and the lower Great Lakes, also revere the Pale God and say his peace religion became such an integral part of their lives, and was based on such sound principles, that their Five-Nation-Confederacy was eventually studied before the Constitution of the United States was written.[3] Thus, the God of the Dawn Light influenced not only local tribes throughout the years but even our latter-day government.

T. J. O' Brien in his *Fair Gods and Feathered Serpents,* comments:

> Whoever this mysterious visitor was, he eventually achieved a high status among the natives, for after the Iroquois gave thanks for all things; in the earth, crops, animals, the sun, the moon, the rain, the stars, each other, they gave special thanks to their revered hero. This they did by placing tobacco leaves upon the ceremonial fire. The smoke an incense from this sacred plant rose slowly upward, creating a path to carry their prayers to the culture hero/creator, who now resides in the heavens holding up the sky as he watches over them. He received their offerings of gratitude and in turn, it was anticipated, would bestow blessings upon them.[4]

In his article regarding *Christ in North America* in *Ancient American Magazine,* Wayne May informs us:

> Native accounts tell of his arrival from the direction of the rising sun, after which he set up a priesthood among his followers, known as the "wau-pa-nu" (the spelling is phonetic). They were said to have healed the sick and instituted new laws. Blood sacrifice was forbidden and replaced by the use of tobacco, today an important element in all traditional Native American ceremonies. Among many eastern tribes, East Star Man is regarded as the Son of the Great Spirit, the Creator.[5]

As the God of the Dawn Light moved from region to region, he taught those he visited in the principles of peaceful civilized living. He also instructed them in religious matters and taught them how to pray. And, in doing so, left them with a legacy so lasting and so powerful that it influenced their behavior from that time forth.

~ ~ ~

Legends reveal that more ominous topics were also included in the Pale God's teachings, for his prophesies have also been retained by many tribes. One such prophecy, which was said to have been imparted by the Pale God atop a temple of painted logs in a place now called Etowa, Georgia, concerned the coming of "the sacrificers" from the south (the Serpents led by the Tortoise). He prophesied further that others would come from the north, along the sunset Ocean, and that a great civil war would commence. So terrible would be the anarchy that followed, that all would take to the forests to preserve their very lives.

He also foretold the coming of white men at a later time, who would come from across the Sunrise Ocean and would take over their broad land.[9] Hansen, tells us that many tribes with the mixed blood of both the Puan and Serpent (the Chocktah, Cherokee, Chickasaw, and Creek) still remember these predictions.

> We remember how He foretold the coming of white man,
> and other predictions. We have backslid from His teachings,
> but to Him we dance the Sun Dance. We remember Great
> Wakona well.[10]

From the legends recounted by various old Indian prophets, we learn that the Pale God taught essentially the same message of love and peace that was taught in the Old World. Unfortunately, only fragments of such sermons have been in retained in their memories, but many recall being taught the "Golden Rule." The Cherokee as well as the Shawnee recall similar teachings.

As would seem consistent with the Savior's gentle nature, he also taught them to honor the animal kingdom. Numerous legends tell of his healing wounded animals along the way as he journeyed from region to region. It was said that even the most ferocious beasts of the forests would lie down at his feet or roll about in front of him in peaceful submission. His peace religion extended to all living creatures, for the Father loves them all.

Along with his message of love and hope, the Prophet also performed miracles and healed the sick. He calmed the seas and quieted the storms, many of which seem to have been of hurricane proportions. Such awe was generated, and such an abundance of love and reverence for him was felt, that all who lived to see the Healer were changed profoundly from that time forth.

~ ~ ~

The Pale God taught the principles of faith, repentance and baptism, to those he visited, and reminded them that the Great Spirit would always smile down upon them if they were righteous, but if they departed from his ways, they would feel his mighty wrath. Occasionally that wrath was felt, such as one experience recounted by Hansen, which tells of a group of Puancee warriors (since known as Pawnee) who formed a band similar in every way to the Gadianton Robbers described in the Book of Mormon. It was a secret league, formed to prey on the country for profit. These young warriors were prepared to return to their old war-religion and the laws of sacrifice that accompanied it. Because they were skeptical of the rumors regarding a Pale God who walked the region, they proceeded with one such sacrifice. Then, before they knew it, a shaft of light pierced the clouds, and within moments the Pale God stood in their midst, and said:

> Is this the way you keep my commandments? Is this the manner of your insult to the Spirit called Tir-aw-wa? I come to shield you from His anger, or lo, great wind would ignite the forest! And to ashes would be consigned the Pawnee Nation![11]

The Pale God then raised the men from the sacrificial flames and stood them on their feet. Upon seeing such an astonishing act, those who had been so quick to doubt his very existence now dropped to their knees in profound repentance and acknowledged his supreme power and majesty. Thus, the Pawnee often tell the story of how the "Son of Mighty Tirawa came back in anger on a shaft of the dawn light" and saved their entire nation from extinction.[12]

Thus the Pale God walked among the scattered of Israel, saving them from themselves and from each other by teaching them the language of peace.

~   ~   ~

Through land after land he journeyed; sometimes by land, sometimes by sea, but always accompanied by many of his disciples. He journeyed tirelessly from village to village and from region to region, teaching all those he encountered in their own language and dialect.

One legend recounted in Hansen's *He Walked the Americas* depicts the Healer's visit to a Sacred City, which lay somewhere to the north of a capital trade center at the point where the Mississippi meets the Missouri. As the Pale God left the merchant ships, which brought him to this destination, the locals bowed in reverence as he made his way slowly past them to the temple. The streets were strewn with flowers in honor of his coming, and it was said "His every move bespoke His kindness" and "His very touch revealed His divinity."

As the legend proceeds, we learn that others from a land called Tollan, which lay far below the Mississippi, came to visit the Pale God, so famous had he become. Apparently "grand preparations were made to receive the emissaries." There were long lines of chanters and elaborate dancers, who were accompanied by conch shell trumpets, flutes, and tom-toms. Ships from several nations were in the procession, but "at last came the beautiful ships of Tollan. From the first ship came the guards all clothed in metal, and then a ship load of glittering musicians playing upon many strange instruments of music." Then came the nobles in their "colored costumes made of colored cotton embroidered with gold, with pearl and emeralds and even their sandals were shining with beauty." They wore "long thick emerald feathers" which "flowed backward like rippling water." These grand strangers greeted the Pale God at the Temple site with "His shining hair" and "snow white mantle." The Pale God received them, and blessed them, and after four days they left, but not before receiving his promise that he would visit their land as well.[13]

His subsequent visit to Tollan, beautiful Tollan, the "golden city," was also memorable. This magnificent city in Central America welcomed him with similar grand processions. Flowers were strewn all across the roadways, just as they had been in the Sacred City along the great Father of Waters far to the north. People came by the hundreds and by the thousands to meet this Pale God who walked among men. There, in the golden city he blessed the people and healed them. He changed their temple rites and organized the priesthood, just as he had done in each of his other stops. To this day, natives recount the legend of that visit to any and all who wish to listen.

~ ~ ~

According to legends, the Dawn God's travels also took him northward into Canada, and then southward again along the West Coast. He came to both the Pueblos and the Havasu where it is said he healed the sick and worked miracles, and even produced water in the otherwise barren deserts.[14] It is said that he also came to the Wallapai and taught them the concepts of peace, and the arts of agriculture. He visited the Hopi and the untamed Seri in the Gulf of Mexico, and taught the Papago to do away with the terrible practice of child sacrifice. He visited the Apache as well, and the Navajo who still refer to him as Yeh-ho-vah.

Thus, the Pale God walked among the scattered of Israel, teaching those same principles that were taught in Jerusalem. He ordained the priesthood, taught baptism rites, and outlawed any form of blood-sacrifice. The Prophet traveled far and wide to reach the lost of Israel and teach them of their Heavenly Father. Then, when his mission was completed, he departed with a promise to one day return.

So greatly did the Yakima in Washington reverence Tacoma, the Healer, that they renamed their highest mountain in honor of his coming.[15] To this day they await his return, for he "promised these sorrowing people that one day through the light of the dawning, He, Tacoma, would return to them."[16] He told the same story to the Polynesians, repeating the message, that he, Wakea, would one day return.[17] Numerous legends from Middle and South America recount essentially the same story, for they, too, had many of Israel among them.

~ ~ ~

Although the Pale God's visit to those in Central and South America reveal that many from Israel occupied those regions, there seems to be a distinction between those who were led to the promised land and those who were directed to the more southern portions of the Hemisphere. Apparently, those who were steeped in idolatry at the time of Israel's dispersion were not allowed to enter the promised land. Only the righteous were given that privilege, for the Lord was determined to preserve a righteous branch of his otherwise corrupted vineyard, and had prepared a land "choice above all others" for their habitat. Thus, because of their idolatrous natures, (for which they were scattered in the first place), many from Israel were denied entrance into the promised land and were directed to Central and South America instead. These lands were still lush and beautiful, but of even more importance, those who entered their borders were not under the same strict command to live righteously or be swept away as those were who entered the promised land. Had it not been so, great numbers would have been destroyed, for their idolatrous practices were an abomination to the Lord. Thus, in his wisdom, and in his efforts to preserve his wayward flock, the Lord directed many from Israel to regions best suited to their individual needs, including Central and South America and the various isles of the sea.

Those few prophets and their families who were led to the land of promise were given a much stricter code to follow, for it was a land especially chosen out of all the world to be a refuge for the righteous. It was destined to be the home of the free, and a place where the foundations of a government would later be laid that would foster the birth of a great nation, one where the restoration of the gospel of Jesus Christ might blossom and where the gathering of the Tribes of Israel from the four corners of the earth might commence. Only those the Lord sanctioned would be permitted within her borders. Moreover, it is for this reason that those who turned to wickedness, after being led to this choice land, were utterly destroyed once they became ripe in iniquity.

The promised land is a holy land and destined for great and marvelous things, including the building up of a "New Jerusalem" in preparation for the Second Advent of the Savior. Even the natives in Missouri are familiar with the events that are to transpire in that region in the latter times. Wayne May, publisher of *Ancient American Magazine,* recounts one such legend for us:

> Long, long ago before the white man arrived, the ancient ones had major trade routes that all crossed at this location which we call today the "Temple Lot". This is the same place dedicated by Joseph Smith, Jr. as the building site for the New Jerusalem, Temple of the restoration. . . .

> Early saints who had settled this area after Joseph's death at Carthage jail, tell us in or near the center of this lot was found a huge stone pile. The Saints and other settlers of the area used this natural resource to build their chimneys, cellars, foundations, fireplaces and for many other constructions needs. The pile was finally removed for street fill in Independence, Missouri.

> As the pile diminished in size, Native Americans were arriving at different times and adding stones to the pile. This continued for about 4 years and then they came no more. It is said that some Indians would walk the streets of the new pioneer settlement looking for their stones and if found they would ask for them back. One such Indian who lived in the area told the following story of the stone pile:

> This area in Missouri was very abundant in wildlife, water, herbs and wild foods which the natives depended on, especially in times of winter. In this region there were major trade routes which were used extensively by a lot of different tribes. It appears a dispute about which tribe was to control the area erupted. When the dispute could not be settled by councils, the beat of war drums seemed to be the only solution. A great gathering of warriors with their chiefs assembled to settle the dispute. As the warriors placed themselves in position, anxious to prove their bravery, they awaited the signal from their war chiefs. Suddenly a personage of glorious light appeared in the middle of the warring tribes. They

stood transfixed and frightened, wondering what sort of sign this was. Then the strange visitor beckoned them to come closer, and sat them down in a council circle. He spoke to their chiefs and told them this was sacred ground, and no blood should ever be shed upon it. The divine visitor told them that they were brothers and should not war one with another. He also told them this was the spot the Great Lodge was to be built. His message was one of peace and they should love one another and live together in peace. He commanded the chiefs to send this message to all the surrounding tribes, and they should make a covenant of peace among themselves. When he finished his teaching, he vanished, as mysteriously as he had appeared.

Those tribes present, in obedience to the command, made peace and a covenant that they would obey the teachings of the Divine Visitor. As a token of their covenant, they placed stones upon this sacred spot to commemorate it. Then to carry out the instructions given them, they dispatched runners to all the surrounding tribes to tell them of this marvelous happening. As the word spread among the other tribes they came each year on the anniversary day to hear the words of the Divine Visitor repeated again. As their token of the covenant, they would bring a stone to place upon what became known as a sacred spot to the various tribes. This is why many of the stones in that pile were not native to Missouri or the immediate surrounding area.[18]

Because of the sacred nature of future events, the command to live righteously or be swept away has always been strictly enforced.

And now, we can behold the decrees of God concerning this land, that it is a land of promise and whatsoever nation shall possess it shall serve God, or they shall be swept off when the fulness of his wrath shall come upon them. And the fulness of his wrath cometh upon them when they are ripened in iniquity. (Ether 2:9)

The Lord was very serious about this edict, and in response, both the Jaredite and the Nephite Nations were totally destroyed when they became fully ripe in iniquity.

~ ~ ~

Although many colonies crossed the great deep at various points in history and landed in a variety of places along the shores of both North and South America, it would certainly not seem unreasonable to suggest there were migrations between continents as well. Especially in light of the fact that there are so many similarities between a few of the tribes on both continents. Cranial types match as well, for the skulls of Mexico's Toltecan family are similar to the skulls of the North American Indians. In MacLean's *The Mound Builders,* we read:

> It has already been stated that the type of the skull, according to certain craniologists, belonged to the Toltecan family. If this be true, then the fact would be established that the Mound Boulders were the original Toltecan race. The Toltecans at an early date settled in Mexico. . . .
>
> From time immemorial there has been immigration into Mexico from the north. One type after another has followed. In some cases different branches of the same family have successively followed one another. Before the Christian Era the Nahoa immigration from the north made its appearance. . . . Certain eminent scientists have held that the Nahoas belonged to the race that made the mounds of the Ohio and Mississippi Valleys. Following this people came the Toltecs, . . . There is a difference of opinion as to the time when the Toltecs entered Mexico. Some argue the date of appearance in Mexico to have been A.D. 648. Clanigero carries it back to the year 596. Other writers appear to make the Nahoas and Toltecs the same and date the time back to 955 B.C. The Toltec monarchy came to an end A.D. 1018. [19]

While many still speculate about just which group of people migrated from the northeast into Mexico and founded the Toltecan race, there is ample evidence to suggest that a people contemporary with either the Jaredite or Nephite nations, or both, migrated southward and mixed with the people in Middle and South America. Thus, many from those regions would naturally carry the blood of Israel in their veins. Therefore, they, too, were entitled to the administration of the Savior when he began his mission among the lost and scattered of Israel. Numerous legends tell of those visitations.

~   ~   ~

So many legends tell the story of a Great White God's visit among the aboriginal races of the New World, that it would be difficult for anyone to dismiss them as mere fanciful tales conjured up by various tribes. At first the Indians were eager to impart such stories to early explorers, but as more and more whites began to scoff at such tales, the Indians refused to share them any longer. Consequently, many have been lost to us. Nonetheless, enough have been recorded by various missionaries and traders among the Indians, over the years, to compile an impressive collection of legends which all tell essentially the same story; the story of a noble man of peace who walked among them and instructed them not only in religious matters, but in matters of agriculture, science and art. So great and lasting was his influence in their lives, that in spite of distortions over the years, the legends of the Pale God's visit among them have been preserved throughout the ages. They tell of a bearded, white man who walked the entire hemisphere proclaiming a universal message of love. One who healed the sick, walked on water, and worked miracles just as Jesus did in the Holy Land; a man so much like the Savior himself, that we might reasonably suggest the two were one and the same; a man who was busy being about his Father's business.

Now, we must be cautious of attributing every legend told of a Great White God's visit to these regions as a visit by the Savior, for some depict an individual who, although apparently on a priestly mission, had attributes not consistent with those of the resurrected Lord. Perhaps such legends were of others who were given the command to preach the gospel, such as the three Nephites who were to tarry until his final coming. Their mission may also have been wondrous, given their priestly powers. Legends of their ministrations may have simply merged with those of the Pales God's over the years, making it seem there was only one Prophet, when, indeed many were commanded to minister among the lost of Israel at that period in time.

The mission of the three Nephites is found in 3 Nephi, where we read:

> And it shall come to pass, when the Lord seeth fit in his wisdom that they shall minister unto all the scattered tribes of Israel, and unto all nations, kindreds, tongues and people, and shall bring out of them unto Jesus many souls, that their desire may be fulfilled, and also because of the convincing power of God which is in them. (3 Ne. 28:29)

~ ~ ~

Because of the visit of the Lord or his emissaries to so many locations in both North and South America, it would not seem unreasonable to assume that a great peace fell upon the entire hemisphere for a time. How long cannot possibly be determined, but the Book of Mormon indicates that, at least in the regions of Book of Mormon territory, peace prevailed for two hundred years. Nations that once sought for each other's blood were friendly to one another, and trade relations were at an all time high, and never were a people happier.

The Savior changed their lives so profoundly that neighbor loved neighbor and each sought the best for each other. In consequence of such devotion, there was no poor among them, no crime, no back biting, and no contention of any kind. But, as is always the case when things are too peaceful, Satan began to stir the pot again and soon their peaceful way of life began to decline.

~ ~ ~

## Notes

1. Hansen, *He Walked the Americas,* 91.
2. O'Brien, *Fair Gods and Feathered Serpents,* 100.
3. Ibid., 101
4. Ibid., 102.
5. May, *Ancient American Magazine,* no. 26, p. 2.
6. Hansen, *He Walked the Americas,* 69.
7. Ibid., 69.
8. Ibid., 48.
9. Ibid., 43.
10. Ibid., 54.
11. Ibid., 58.
12. Ibid., 59.
13. Ibid., 84.
14. Ibid., 92.
15. Ibid., 86.
16. Ibid.
17. Ibid., 87.
18. Wayne May, publisher of *Ancient American Magazine.* Sources: Cecil Abbott and Richard Hensley of the Indian Ministry Council of the Americas, Blue Springs, Mo.; William Sheldon, Church of Jesus Christ (Temple Lot), Independence, Mo.; Angela Wheaton, *Zion's Advocate* (August 1964): 117.
19. Baldwin, *Ancient America,* 148–49.

Chapter Eleven

# The End of an Era

The years following the Savior's visit to Bountiful were so filled with love, that the entire population enjoyed a time of peace unknown before that time. The Spirit rained down upon them in such rich abundance that they became a Zion people, and never were they happier. But, time has a way of diminishing our memories, and although those who witnessed the Savior's appearance never forgot that marvelous experience, it was difficult to impress upon the minds of the upcoming generations the magnificence of that sacred occurrence. Consequently, the rising generations grew cold and indifferent to the stories told them by their parents and grandparents. And, as is always the case when prosperity becomes the norm, they soon became steeped in pride and began to worship the workmanship of their own hands again and to seek for riches. Worst of all, they began to make idols and to dabble in works of darkness and became a wicked and perverse people, building up the "high places" of old for evil and unholy purposes. Thus, those in the latter-days who try to piece together the complicated puzzle of the Hopewellian Epoch have an assortment of earthen works scattered across the mound building region that leave us much to ponder. Were they built up to honor the Lord, Jesus Christ, or were they built up to any number of strange deities concocted by the wicked who, after conquering territory after territory, interjected their own perverse traditions upon the conquered? Moreover, both the Nephites and Lamanites were so steeped in wickedness by the end of the third century A.D., they both would have used these structures for unholy purposes. Therefore, those of our modern age who believe many of these monuments seem to reek of idolatry are probably right.

In light of this dilemma, it would be nearly impossible to determine the true purpose for many of the mounds, simply because one culture over lapped another beginning as far back as the beginning of the woodland epoch. Archeological findings can only tell us so much about that ancient era. Likewise, legends and traditions can only tell us so much. In fact, even the scriptures can only tell us so much, for they contain the history of such a limited portion of the eastern woodlands.

Although years of of research and investigation have provided much information regarding that ancient era, the sudden and complete disappearance of the Hopewellian culture around A.D. 400 still mystifies the world, and much speculation about their extinction has arisen. William Henry Harrison, (later to be ninth President of the United States) had his own opinion about the disappearance of the Mound Builders, as we learn from Silverberg's account of him,

> He imagined stirring battles, sweeping migrations of tribes under attack, mighty swarms of civilized people streaming the headland of what one day would be the United States of America. To learn of them he wrote ". . . We must learn first, from the extensive country covered by their remains, that they were a numerous people. Secondly, that they were congregated in considerable cities. . . . Thirdly, that they were essentially an agricultural people; because, collected as they were in great numbers, they

could have depended on the chase {hunting} but for a small portion of their subsistence.' He was of the opinion that the Mound Builders 'were compelled to fly from a more numerous or a more gallant people. No doubt the contest was long and bloody. . . ."

Archeological evidence reveals much about the ultimate disappearance of the Hopewellian people, but it will be within the pages of the Book of Mormon that we will find the greatest amount of information about that dark time. For example, in 4 Nephi, we learn how corrupt both the Nephites and Lamanites had become just three hundred years following the Savior's visit. Moreover, we can follow their battles from city to city and from land to land until the whole Nephite nation met their complete demise at the hands of the wicked Lamanites around A.D. 400.

Physical evidence of those long and bloody battles has been found all across western New York. Artifacts of war have been gathered up by the armfuls, and thousands upon thousands of bones have been discovered in pits and mounds throughout the region. Nowhere else in the United States are relics of ancient warfare more prevalent than in the regions surrounding the Hill Cumorah. And, nowhere else is there more evidence that an entire civilization collapsed at the precise time ascribed to the extinction of the Nephite nation in the Book of Mormon.

Because of such overwhelming evidence of warfare, MacLean believed the eventual disappearance of the Hopewellian culture came about by force from invading armies from the north. Although, according to the drama played out in the Book of Mormon his theory is reversed, his observations are very astute, for archeological evidence makes it clear that warfare preceded their extinction. Strong fortifications dot the countryside and mounds erected on hilltops were thought to be used as observation posts to scan for any approaching invasion. In spite of such apparent preparations, however, MacLean believed the final overthrow, or expulsion of the Mound Builders was sudden and complete around A.D. 400.

Fortunately, the scriptures provide a more detailed account of their ultimate demise. They inform us there was a division among the people once again, with the righteous calling themselves Nephites and the wicked taking the name Lamanites. We learn further, that during those final years the righteous began to gather together their forces under the direction of the Mormon and his son Moroni. They gathered any and all who were not affiliated with the Lamanites to the land of many waters where they set up camp and began to make preparations for the greatest battle of their lives If they were victorious, it would mean the return of their lands. But, if they lost, it would mean the end of them all. For four long years they gathered any and all who were called Nephites to the lands surrounding the Hill Cumorah and prepared for the up coming conflict. Then, when the battle cries were finally sounded, one of the most terrible battles of all time commenced and continued until the blood of that entire nation was spilled upon the ground. The Lamanites had come down upon them in such fury and in such great numbers that the entire Nephite nation was totally and completely destroyed. Thus, quite suddenly, a

The Hill Cumorah, scene of the final battle.
Courtesy The Church of Jesus Christ of Latter-day Saints.

civilization that thrived in the region for nine hundred years became extinct; only the Lamanites remained.

Now, even though the Book of Mormon contains the answer so many seek, the reason for the sudden and abrupt end of the Hopewellian Culture still seems to be a mystery to the world. Rather than accept the history contained in the Book of Mormon, however, some simply speculate that a plague may have wiped them out or perhaps unrelenting drought or pestilence of some kind. However, because so many hilltop enclosures which were obviously meant for defense have been found throughout the mound building regions, most authorities recognize that warfare was probably the cause of their disappearance (just as the Book of Mormon tells us it was).

Such conclusions were reached, in part, because archeologists noted the ceremonial centers in the Ohio River Valley did not appear to have been fortified and no evidence of warfare could be found around them. Thus, they speculated that they had been built up during times of peace. The hilltop enclosures or "forts," on the other hand, had much evidence of warfare. Therefore, it was concluded that they were built up during times of trouble. The fact these enclosures were built in inaccessible locations bordered by hills or near steep cliffs, further solidified that supposition. Lingering evidence of great fires owing to possible attacks upon the forts along with piles of bones buried within the enclosure, helped strengthened that premise.

Evidence also indicates that just prior to the demise of the Hopewellian people, mound centers in Ohio and fortified cities in New York were being abandoned as their populations began to flee from invading forces. It was obvious to all who examined the scene that something terrible was happening in both New York and the Ohio Valley at this point in history; so terrible, in fact, that it is thought to have precipitated the complete extinction of the entire Hopewellian civilization. For that reason the enclosures in Ohio were labeled "terminal Hopewell." Not surprisingly, archeological evidence indicates that

Hopewell in New York disappeared as suddenly as those in Ohio, which Prufer, of the Case Institute of Technology, considers proof of a direct connection between these two regions.

We might remember that during the Book of Mormon era, the Nephites were instructed by the Lord that they must never make the first strike against the Lamanites. However, during these final days of tribulation, all bets were off, and the Nephites were just as aggressive as the Lamanites. By this time one side was just as wicked as the other. Prufer, comments on that terrible time:

> Hopewell went through a long and piecemeal degeneration which may have lasted from 200 to 500 years, ending, perhaps, about A.D. 450. During this decline there seemed to have been an end to wide-spread trade relations and a resulting disappearance of foreign and exotic materials. There was also a decline in the importance of building large mounds and ceremonial enclosures and placing of large amounts of grave offerings with burials. . . . The end result of this decline, in Late Woodland times, was a population. . . which had in many respects returned to the localized tribal way of living which had exited before Hopewell. Practically all remnants of the great Hopewell culture and its economic and artistic inspiration were abandoned. . . . The same precess seems to have gone on in all parts of the wide-spread Hopewell territory.'[1]

As the Hopewellian culture began to decline, so did mound building, ceremonialism, and long-distance trading networks, and by A.D. 400, their distinctive way of life was over. The awful scenes of horror and bloodshed that spread across the land at the close of that era, were described for us in the Book of Mormon.

> And it came to pass that my people, with their wives and their children, did now behold the armies of the Lamanites marching towards them; and with that awful fear of death which fills the breasts of all the wicked, did they await to receive them.

> And it came to pass that they came to battle against
> us, and every soul was filled with terror because of the
> greatness of their numbers. (Morm. 6:7–8)

As the on-going wars of extinction continued, fortifications began to dot the hillsides as each side struggled for sur-
vival against the frenzied rage of opposing armies. The war
was terrible. Words cannot describe it. Never has such a scene
presented itself to us. And all because they had turned from the
ways of the Lord and embraced the unholy ways of the Evil
One instead. The words of Moroni, the last Nephite survivor
of the Nephite nation, are heart wrenching.

> And my soul was rent with anguish, because of the
> slain of my people, and I cried:
>
> O ye fair ones, how could ye have departed from
> the ways of the Lord! O ye fair ones, how could ye
> have rejected that Jesus, who stood with open arms to
> receive you!
>
> Behold, if ye had not done this, ye would not have
> fallen. But behold, ye are fallen, and I mourn your loss.
>
> O ye fair sons and daughters, ye fathers and mothers,
> ye husbands and wives, ye fair ones, how is it that ye could
> have fallen!
>
> But behold, ye are gone, and my sorrows cannot bring
> your return. (Morm. 6:17–20)

After four hundred years had passed away from the time
of the Savior's visit among them, the Nephite civilization
came to a complete and abrupt end, and the remaining victorious Lamanites dissolved into wandering tribes.

Because the Nephites had turned from the ways of the
Lord after having enjoyed so many great and spiritual blessings, they were not permitted to remain in the promised land
and, thus, met their Maker that fateful day. Not so with the
Lamanites, for they had received promises that they would not
be utterly destroyed along with their Nephite brethren because

of their devotion to the word once they had been enlightened, and because of promises made to early prophets in their behalf. Therefore, the Lord was more lenient with them, especially since they were only living those laws that had been handed down by their fathers.

> For there are many promises which are extended to the Lamanites; for it is because of the traditions of their fathers that caused them to remain in their state of ignorance; therefore the Lord will be merciful unto them and prolong their existence in the land. (Alma 9:16)

In consequence of these blessings, the Lamanites were not utterly destroyed along with their Nephite brethren, but would continue to walk the promised land until the time of European contact, and beyond. The time will come, however, when the Lord will teach them of their history as contained in the Book of Mormon, and they will return to the God of their ancient fathers and embrace his gospel of love.

> After my seed and the seed of my brethren shall have dwindled in unbelief, and shall have been smitten by the Gentiles; yea, after the Lord God shall have camped against them round about, and shall have laid siege against them with a mount, and raised forts against them; and after they shall have been brought down low in the dust, even that they are not, yet the words of the righteous shall be written, and the prayers of the faithful shall be heard, and all those who have dwindled in unbelief shall not be forgotten.
>
> For those who shall be destroyed, shall speak unto them out of the ground and their speech shall be low out of the dust, and their voice shall be as one that hath a familiar spirit. (2 Ne. 26:15–16)

Not only did the entire Nephite nation perish "amid the yells of their enemies" during that terrible war, but many of the Lamanites died as well. Thus, a culture called "Hopewellian" faded into oblivion. Only the last to survive the Lamanite Nation remained.

For a time the land was silent except for the distant drums that called rival tribes together in battle after battle as each vied for territory and dominion. But, the sounds of bustling mound centers and excited village life ceased to be heard in the woodlands ever after, for many of the Lamanites moved from that blood-splattered land and into those regions further to the south. Ruins over-grown with centuries of forest growth are all that remain of that once thriving civilization.

~ ~ ~

Time passed, and still the land was silent. Then, as their numbers grew again, a new culture grew up around A.D. 700, called, the Mississippian Epoch, so named because many ruins from that culture are found along the Mississippi River. It stretched from Wisconsin to the Gulf of Mexico, as well as in the south, occupying regions stretching westward from Georgia through Tennessee, Ohio, Illinois, Arkansas, and Texas to Oklahoma.

Kneeling man from Temple Mound, Tennessee. Courtesy Frank H. McClung Museum, University of Tennessee, Knoxville, Tennessee.

Because the ceremonial centers built up during that period were different from those built during the Hopewellian Epoch, many have questioned whether a different culture may have entered the picture at that point in time. In fact, because their pyramidal temples resembled those found in Mesoamerica, some speculated that some kind of intercourse had taken place

171

between the Lamanites and those tribes from the regions of Central America or Mexico. Although the new school of though discounts that notion altogether, legends often speak of trade relations between the two continents.

Another legend recounted by Hansen in *He Walked the Americas* tells of a major invasion from the south, which may just answer the question of why the mounds in the southern regions differed so dramatically from those in the Ohio Valley during the earlier Hopewellian Era. This invasion did not come from either Mexico or Central America but, nonetheless, did come from the south. Apparently an island existed somewhere in southern waters which has long since disappeared into the ocean. The legend has it that as their land became scarcer and scarcer due to storms and great earthquakes, the people living upon this island took to the mountains. Unfortunately, one tribe among them vied for dominance over their entire population. Rather than become servants to one of their own, many took to their boats and sailed up the great Father of Waters, the Mississippi River, and took possession of much of the southern regions of the promised land by force. Shortly thereafter, the Serpents, as they were called, "keepers of the books and learning," built the great Serpent Mound to commemorate their entrance into the land.

Now, apparently, he who sired their tribe had visions of grandeur and desired to unite all the kingdoms from the sunrise ocean to the sunset ocean. In fact, according to legend, he may have succeeded in his desire, but Northmen from the West Coast destroyed his armies, and warfare broke out all over the empire just as predicted by the great Pale God, Waicomah, centuries earlier. The people were forced to abandoned their cities and entered the forests for protection as war after war dominated the ensuing years.

Legends told by the old Indian De-coo-dah, tell of many divisions of succeeding nations. They tell of family rivalries, including numerous assassinations and major revolutions.

Consequently, after centuries of conflict, their empires were completely broken up just prior to the arrival of Columbus. Thus, the Lamanites of the past had been demoralized and walked as simple hunter-gatherers at the time of European contact. Fortunately, their histories have been written in the earth and kept in legends, and speak of a time far distant when the Lamanites walked as great warriors throughout the land.

During those earlier years, mounds continued to be built, some for good, some for bad, but by the Mississippian Era, most were relegated to false forms of worship. Regarding such worship we read:

> Atop them elaborate rituals that involved a belief in an upper and a lower world may have been conducted, drawing participants from all over the local region and helping confer on them a common identity.[2]

Every indication suggests these were a superstitious people, steeped in idolatry and sin. Once they became steeped in wickedness the Spirit of the Lord withdrew, and the Evil One quickly stepped in and provided various idolatrous forms of worship, which held the people together and gave them something greater than self to believe in.

Antoine Le Page de Pratz, a Dutch settler in the Louisiana Colony in the 1700s, recorded many of the Mississippi Natchez Indian legends and gives the following account of such a belief system:

> The supreme ruler of the Natchez, was the Great Sun, a living deity believed to be a direct descendant or even the actual brother of the sun itself. He was assisted by a supreme war chief, his own earthly brother Tattooed Serpent, and a number of other immediate Sun family members including Women suns—his mother and sisters. Beneath them in the administrative hierarchy were the chiefs of the seven individual districts, or satellites villages. These men and other high officials were lessor relatives of the Great Sun, and highly respected as members of the first family. A notch lower on the scale were the Nobles, then the Honored Men;

and much lower, the commoners, who did the less-than-glorious work of procuring food for their masters and hauling baskets of soil to top off the mounds. These wretches, according to Europeans, were known by the Natchez language equivalent of stinkers, or stinkards.[3]

The great Sun of the Natchez Tribes lived atop the Temple Mound in the tribes' administrative centers or villages. Settlements spread out from there. The Sun's power was absolute and his subjects were quick to observe his wishes, as further explained by Pratz.

> Fathers of families never fail to bring to the temple the first fruits of everything they gather, and they do the same by all the presents that are made to the nation. They expose them at the door of the temple, the keeper of which after having presented them to the spirits carries them to the great chief, who distributes them to whom he pleased."[4]

In spite of all investigations regarding distant lands and ancient civilizations, nothing reveals more about a people than their religion. Thus, the similarities between this practice with certain observances in the Law of Moses gives us some idea of their earlier religious foundations. They apparently still believed in an afterlife and still understood the glorious state of those who entered that heavenly realm. In fact, so imbedded was that belief that many willingly went to their death just to get there, such as this example told Pratz by the Natchez:

> When the body of Tattooed Serpent had lain in state for the allotted time, elaborately clothed and painted and wearing moccasins for his journey, his fellow travelers were escorted to death mats outside the temple. With deerskins placed over their heads, they were strangled with cords. Not an attractive prospect for even the most enthusiastic volunteer, but wives above all were willing to face it. They were convinced of an other-world life far better than the earthly life they knew. Tattooed Serpent's favorite wife, shortly before the end, tried to explain to du Pratz and his company that they should not mourn the war chief or his family and

Monks Mound at Cahokia, Illinois,
overlooking the Grand Plaza and the Twin Mounds.
Courtesy Cahokia Mounds State Historic Site.
Painting by William R. Iseminger.

friends: "What does it matter? He is in the country of the spirits, and in two days I will go to join him and will tell him that I have seen your hearts shake at the sight of his dead body. Do not grieve. We will be friends for a much longer time in the country of the spirits than in this, because one does not die there again. It is always fine weather, one is never hungry, and men do not make war there any more.[5]

Mounds of gigantic size filled the southern regions of the United States during the Mississippian Epoch. Huge, pyramidal structures that amazed all who gazed upon them. These large, flat topped mounds were built as foundations for their temples and for the elevated residence of their most prominent chiefs, and have since been named Temple Mounds by modern archeologists. The natives apparently lived in small villages surrounding the mounds and were a combined hunting and farming people, who observed a strange cult of the dead.

The largest of these temple mounds is found in Cahokia, Illinois, which attained its greatest prominence around A.D. 1100. This center, which measures some five-and-a-half square miles, is so large it rivals some cities in Europe and may have been populated by as many as ten thousand to twenty thousand people. Then, as mysteriously as the Mississippian Culture came into existence, it suddenly disappeared; possibly in the same way the Nephite nation disappeared—as a result of wickedness and warfare. The Lord's patience will only extend so far before he prunes his vineyard again.

Nevertheless, even though the grand centers disappeared, a number of smaller sub-regional centers continued to occupy the Mississippi regions until the time of European contact. Little by little, the Lamanites digressed in power and dominion until they were eventually reduced to the state of wandering nomads. Thus, tribal wars and idolatry cost them dearly over the centuries.

Regardless of the mounting evidence that a superior culture once occupied the woodlands, many modern day authorities are still convinced the Indians alone built the mounds and not some lost race as so many have supposed. Especially after Cyrus Thomas of the Bureau of Ethnology claimed, "the links discovered directly connecting the Indians and mound builders are so numerous and well established that there should no longer be any hesitancy in accepting the theory that the two are one and the same people." He never supposed for a moment that both the Indians and still another culture, who have since been lost through time, participated in the building up of the Hopewellian culture.

The mounds and the lost race who built them have been all but forgotten with the passing of time. Moreover, the efforts of those who have tried to discount any and all evidence that supports the premise that a superior race once occupied the region have succeeded for a time, but only for a time, for the Lord will ultimately manifest the truth of all things to those who diligently seek for truth and knowledge. Thus, we can rest assured that in the Lord's good time, the remnants of that lost civilization will find their place in history and the bones of their dead will rest in peace at last.

~ ~ ~

## Notes

1. Prufer, *Hopewellian Studies,* 54–55.
2. *Mound Builders & Cliff Dwellers,* 46.
3. Ibid., 48.
4. Ibid., 49.
5. Ibid., 50.

De-Coo-Da

Chapter Twelve

# Legends of the Mounds

Because of major religious differences, the Nephites had an entirely different culture than the Lamanites. It was built upon righteous principles and a clear understanding of those scriptures which were carried with them across the great waters at the time they left Jerusalem. They lived the Law of Moses and were given instructions regularly. Therefore, the Nephites understood the history of God's dealing with his people from the beginning of time, including the Creation, the Great Deluge and all the prophecies concerning the coming of a Messiah.

The Lamanites, on the other hand, were deprived of those sacred records, for they left the family unit early in their sojourn in the promised land. Moreover, because of wickedness, the Spirit withdrew from them. Consequently, their views of religion became distorted over the years and they became a wicked and an idolatrous people. Under such circumstances, the Evil One was only too quick to show them an alternative religion meant to satisfy their need for worship, but also meant to lead them astray. He encouraged class distinction as well.

They catered to the elite among them while the lower classes lived in tents and in small farming communities along the river bottoms not far from the ruling mound centers.

Regardless of such religious and cultural distortions, a great many changes took place among the Lamanites after the Savior's visit. The outpouring of the Spirit was so strong at that time, the Lamanites set aside their old perverted traditions and began to worship Jehovah instead. But, as time passed and the Hopewellian era began to decline, those sacred enclosures, which were once used to worshiped the Savior, were no longer used for such holy purposes but were used, instead, for more idolatrous practices—including human sacrifice. Thus, the mounds found scattered across the woodlands were used for a variety of purposes, some righteous and some not. Unfortunately, because such edifices are so foreign to our present understanding, we have no way to determine the purposes for which many were built. We must turn to legends and to the traditions handed down by Indian holy men over the years for some indication of their original use.

William Pidgeon, a trader among the Indians who was concerned the legends of the Native Americans would eventually be lost, made the following comment:

> From the remotest antiquity, nations and their rulers have vied with each other in their efforts to erect memorials of themselves which should withstand the ravages of time, and by their colossal proportions, costliness, or rare beauty, impress coming ages with a conviction of the greatness and power of the builders. The pyramids of Egypt, the mighty columns of Balbee, the palace walls of Yucatan, all tell the same story. But it has not seldom happened, in the word's history, that the monument has outlasted the memory of its builder or its tenant, of the nation which erected it, or of the event it was designed to commemorate. The sculpture or the paintings upon its wall, and the hieroglyphics which are supposed to record its history, speak an unknown tongue, and only dim tradition can aid us to guess their origin and import. It is only within a very recent period that the

attentive study of the Egyptian antiquities has been rewarded
by a discovery of the key to the hieroglyphic writings; and
yet more recently, the sculptured walls of buried cities are
beginning to reveal secrets lost for ages, and to tell of populous nations and mighty sovereigns, whose very names
had been unknown for centuries. But while the antiquities
of the Old World are deservedly attracting so much attention from scholars and antiquarians, ought those of our own
country to be forgotten or overlooked? And ought the earth-
work memorials of the mound builders, presenting (as we
believe) some of the earliest and most primitive forms of
hieroglyphic records, to receive their due share of attention,
as the source of all which now remains to us of the history
of an extinct race?[1]

Although most Indian Nations claim no memory of the
origin of the mounds, one old Indian named De-coo-dah,
keeper of his tribe's traditions, had much to say about them to
Pidgeon who subsequently published a book entitled *Traditions of De-Coo-Dah,* in 1858. While many scoffed at this old
Indian's "fanciful tales," others have since begun to give his
remarks "a measure of scientific respectability."[2]

According to Pidgeon, De-coo-dah "claimed no lineal
kindred with any nation now in existence, but claimed to be a
descendant from the Elk Nation, now extinct." He said, "they
were a mixed nation, claiming descent from those ancient
Americans, the Mound Builders; and that their traditions were
sacredly kept by their prophets, from a family of whom he was
descended:"[3] As the last survivor of that nation, he alone carried the legends he subsequently told Pidgeon regarding the
mounds and the supposed purposes of many.

As his teachings began, he informed Pidgeon that many
mounds were simply signs that conveyed ideas in their various
forms or shapes, "and their different significations could only
be known by vocal instruction." He went on to say that many
contained "the relics of kings, prophets, and great chiefs, which
had been gathered together and deposited in strata from time

to time until the monument was full. Then, the process began all over again and a new cemetery commenced. Thus, from the legends and traditions handed down by his fathers, De-coo-dah began to pass down the history of the mounds, many of which date back to times of great antiquity.

~ ~ ~

Now, because so many authorities continued to believe the mounds were built by the descendants of the Indians, it would seem perfectly reasonable to suggest that by going to such Indian historians we might gather bits of history regarding the mounds. But, not surprisingly, even the tales of this well-respected old prophet were referred to as "pure nonsense." In fact, T. Lewis, a surveyor who surveyed some of Pidgeon's supposed sites, went so far as to declare, "The Elk Nation and its last prophet De-coo-dah are modern myths, which have never had any objective existence; and that, consequently the ancient history in the volume [*Traditions of De-Coo-Dah*] is of no more account than that of the Lost Tribes in the Book of Mormon."[4]

In spite of such a cutting denunciation of Pidgeon's work, the legends of De-coo-dah are incredibly detailed. They give us information that could have come from no other source, for other keepers of such the legends have long since passed away. Thus, the history of the mounds, along with their origins and purposes, were all destined to be forgotten with the passing of their last living prophet, De-coo-dah.

~ ~ ~

De-coo-dah was nearly ninety years of age when he met and befriended William Pidgeon. It took some time for this grand old gentlemen to trust Pidgeon, but their friendship ultimately became so strong and lasting De-coo-dah ultimately adopted him. Toward the end of his own life he made the following concession:

I am very old, and must soon sleep with my fathers to be remembered no more.

I have no son to perpetuate my memory, or transit to posterity what yet remains of ancient tradition.

I have never trusted any white man with the traditions that I have imparted to you; receive them as the words of truth, and keep them as a sacred trust.

You have treated me with kindness without the hope of reward. I have nothing to leave you in return that will call to your remembrance our mutual friendship, save those ancient traditions. Treasure them, then, in your paper-book, and keep them as the dying gift of De-coo-dah; and when you return to your father, your children and friends, these will furnish matter of interesting conversation for you all. And when you or they look upon any of these ancient works, they will, perhaps, recall to your remembrance your friend the old Mocking-Bird [a nickname given him in childhood].[5]

Knowing his grandfathers held such reverence for the mounds, De-coo-dah proceeded to explain the history of many to Pidgeon in an effort to keep their origins and purposes alive for posterity. He began by explaining the mounds were not as mysterious as many had supposed, but were simply built to commemorate national events such as royal marriages, royal births, valorous achievements, or other special events. He explained that,"a new mound was erected at each national festival;" and at that time "each nation erected a national monument significant of their number and dignity."[6] Consequently, some mounds were quite spectacular.

Mounds were also used to mark the sites of population centers and were used as hieroglyphic forms of writing to record the history of each city. They were to be read from the inside out, with the mounds in the center and the cities swirling out about them. One such city was said to have had an even longer history than our modern-day London.

Legends reveal a large capital city near the entrance of the Missouri River had "boulevards radiating outward like the spokes of a giant wheel." From the central hub Crest Mounds recorded the ages of the ancient Puant Nation.

> On the Crests stood the Capitol Buildings, built of great logs and beautifully painted, as was Puant custom. On the sides of the Crests were earth-hugging strawberry carpets, mosaiced and bordered with garlands of flowers.[7]

Tradition has it that many great cities spread out across the eastern woodlands—each with a recorded beginning and an end.

> When a dynasty has been completed, and a Calendar Period ended, the artifacts of the period, the significant facts pictured on pottery, were placed within, and the Crest was closed with a Mound of Extinction. Henceforth this one was not to be reopened, and beyond it was built a new Crest for the new period.[8]

According to De-coo-dah, conquering nations never destroyed the histories of the conquered nation but simply added to them. Consequently, these complicated historical monuments have remained in the land for centuries.

Because of the degenerate state of the Indians at the time of European contact, some authorities have questioned whether the Indians were industrious enough to have created such stupendous works, supposing, as they did, that the Indians had always been adverse to such laborious work. Nevertheless, the scriptures inform us that only the more idle Lamanites lived off the land during the Nephite era, while others apparently lived in homes and cities and their kings were said to have lived in palaces (see Alma 22:2). We can assume, therefore, that a great many Indians, although not in the enlightened state of their Nephite brethren, nonetheless lived in organized societies under the political rule of various kings.

We might also remember that when the sons of Mosiah entered Lamanite territory to preach the gospel, they went to a "great city." It had been built by the combined efforts of the Lamanites, the Amalakites and the people of Amulon, which they called Jerusalem after the name of their father's nativity (see Alma 21:1–2). The Lamanites often shared their territories with dissenters from the Nephites. Some even became their leaders and even their kings such as Amalickiah and his brother Ammoron. Consequently, their strength and ingenuity were undoubtedly used to strengthen those regions, and the Lamanites often prospered under their rule. Apparently, it was not until after the slaughter of the Nephites at Cumorah that the Lamanites as a whole degenerated to the primitive state early explorers found them in centuries later.

> This people shall be scattered, and shall become a dark and a loathsome people, beyond the description of that which ever hath been amongst us, yea, even that which hath been among the Lamanites, and this because of their unbelief and idolatry. (Morm. 5:15)

During the Nephite era, many Lamanites were industrious enough to have built up societies which prospered to some degree and may well have produced the earthen-works and artifacts which have subsequently been found and labeled part of the "Adena Culture." They even learned the written language of the Nephites.

> But they taught them that they should keep their record, and that they might write one to another.
>
> And thus the Lamanites began to increase in riches, and began to trade one with one another and wax great, and began to be a cunning and a wise people, as to the wisdom of the world, yea, a very cunning people, delighting in all manner of wickedness and plunder, except it were among their own brethren. (Mosiah 24:6–7)

Even so, they most often used this written language for the purpose of bartering with one another and not for the purpose of keeping their histories. Evidently, their hieroglyphic form of writing served that purpose. De-coo-dah explains further:

The face of the earth is the red-man's book, and these mounds and embankments are some of his letters; I am but a poor scholar, but I will try to read for you as well as I can, the letters we have been viewing today. You are aware that when the white man reads, he begins at the edge of his book; when you read the red-man's book, begin in the center.

He continued:

You observe in the center of this group, a large mound with no small mound near it; this once stood in the center of an ancient city, the home of a great king. The space between it and the smaller mounds, was once covered with wigwams. This central monument was called the king's tower, and was daily used as a place of look-out. The smaller mounds, with the exception of the four that we first visited, are national memorials; the inner circle memorialized the race of legitimate sovereigns, ancestors of the founder of this metropolis; the second circle memorializes, numerically, the great chiefs that signalized themselves during their reign of those sovereigns; and the outer circles give the number of loyal tribes under the control of the founder of the metropolis at the time of its erection, each tribe constructing its own monument. Thus you read in these letters the rise and progress of a great nation under the sovereignty of twelve kings, sustained by sixteen great war-chiefs, commanding forty-four tribes. The four residential, or large mounds, that surround the inner circles, were occupied by dignitaries in power during the primitive occupancy of the metropolis. The north residential was occupied by the king, the south by the commanding war-chiefs, the eastern by the prince entitled to succession, and the western by the holy prophet.[9]

From this description, we can see just how complicated this form of hieroglyphic writing actually was.

~   ~   ~

After extensive explorations of the mound building region, it becomes apparent that different cultures expressed themselves in a variety of ways, which is evidenced by the fact the earthen works found in various parts of the region often differ considerably. Effigy mounds, (those that resemble animals or humans) are most frequently found in Wisconsin and its vicinity, while geometrical designs are almost exclusively found in Ohio. Mounds of every conceivable size

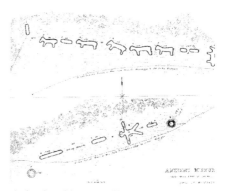

Animal and human effigy mounds found in Dade County, Wisconsin. Squier and Davis, Ancient Monuments, 1848.

and shape can be found all over the mound building region.

Although earthworks are found on all major rivers in the area, the greatest concentrations have been found along the Ohio River. Southern Ohio is considered the heart of the Hopewell Culture and has the most elaborate of all the earthworks in the region. Many are stupendous and much speculation about their origins and purposes have surfaced over the years, but none more interesting than the purposes ascribed by De-coo-dah.

In commenting on the impressive earthen works in Circleville, Ohio, with its circles and squares (which Atwater believed indicated its builders had been master surveyors), De-coo-dah said:

> This is one of the most ancient sacred structures known. Here was the great storehouse of ancient tradition; here many sacred rites and ceremonies had their origin; and the wilful transgression of laws and edits here promulgated was punished with death. Many moons were spent in the construction of this great work. With the earth of the central mound were mingled the ashes of dead prophets, gathered together from the four nations. The ashes of infants helped to rear the matrimonial mounds, and the remains of many generations formed a part of the wall of the inner circle.

187

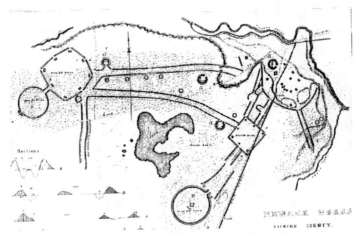

Newark Works, Licking County, Ohio.
Squier and Davis, *Ancient Monuments,* 1848.

This was the work rendered sacred by the materials employed in its construction. But the exterior wall was formed of earth thrown from the ditch which surrounds the inner circle.[10]

Another enclosure considered sacred in nature is situated near Newark, Ohio, and occupies an area of nearly four miles square. It has three principle divisions connected by walls and smaller works. Squier was particularly impressed with this complicated enclosure and said:

> Here, covered with gigantic trees of a primitive forest, the work presents a truly grand and impressive appearance; and, in entering the ancient avenue for the first time, the visitor does not fail to experience a sensation of awe, such as he might feel in passing the portals of an Egyptian temple, or in gazing upon the silent ruins of Petra of the desert.[11]

Atwater was of the opinion that this particular work was primarily for defensive purposes, which he described as a

> large eight sided "fort" and its adjoining circular enclosure. . . . The octagon in his day covered some 40 acres, with

walls about 10 feet high. Eight openings 5 feet wide pierced the walls, with a small mound of earth in front of each. Nearby was the 22 acre circular "fort" and at a greater distance was another large circular enclosure with what Atwater considered a square "fort" beside it.[12]

De-coo-dah assigns this enclosure a different purpose, however. In fact, a "totally" different purpose.

> This work is traditionally represented to have been a prophet's metropolis, or holy seminary of priests or prophets, with its holy circles, festival square, secluded walks, private avenues, sacred residentials, heavenly clusters, and funeral piles.
>
> The five residential circles were permanent abodes of the senior fathers, who were appointed by the people to impart instruction to the junior prophets. These latter inhabited, in common, the pyramidal mounds within the octagon. To the octagon is appended a holy festival circle, known as such by its peculiar manner of construction, being formed with two avenues, the one from without, and the other communicating with the octagon. Upon the pyramidal altar adjacent to the cluster of symbols of deities, was consumed the evening sacrifice offered at the appearance of each new moon."[13]

Another group of works considered a sacrificial pentagon was found in Wisconsin and has elicited a number of theories in regards to its use. However, De-coo-dah tells us:

> The central mound is represented to have been the most holy sacrificial altar known to tradition and the peculiar form of the surrounding works show it to have been of the highest order of sacrificial monuments, and dedicated to the offering of human sacrifice only.
>
> The five small mounds within the pentagon were denominated oracular mounds; and one being set apart to each prophet; they frequently retired there to receive oracular counsel, which, from the summit of the mound at the entrance to the great circle, they subsequently delivered to the people. The five prophets set apart for this service were

in continual attendance; their wants being administered to by the people.

The times of offering was in the spring and the fall, and it was the oldest male's privilege to offer his head in sacrifice. [14]

Along with such impressive works including those erected as title, amalgamation, sacred, and various effigy mounds, there

were also works set apart for the festivals. De-coo-dah informed Pidgeon, that even though a "Festival Circle" was the property of just one nation it was used in common by all. It was a time of entertainment and an abundance of food was always provided at these annual festivals, and tradition has it they were scenes of great merriment. Apparently, one could tell the strength of a nation from the dimensions of its festival circle.

Burial mounds. Squier and Davis, *Ancient Monuments,* 1848.

Matrimonial circles were also prevalent. During the annual feasts, the resident prophet occupied the summit of the prophet's matrimonial altar from day-dawn to sunrise, and from sunset until the close of twilight. At these times, those wishing to unite in matrimony might appear at the matrimonial altar dedicated to the nations of which they were members. [15]

~  ~  ~

Of course, burial mounds are by far the most numerous of all the mounds and they dot the entire countryside. De-coo-dah instructed Pidgeon that separate nations buried their dead in various manners, including cremation. He taught him further that each family had a sacred circle that was considered

First burial in Adena Mound.
Thomas, *12th Annual Report of the Bureau of Ethnology.*

the resting place for their dead. As each member died they were placed in the circle, and after preparing fuel, the body was burned. Then the ashes were covered with earth. The same procedure took place as each succeeding death occurred until the sacred circle was filled. The ring was then raised about two feet and the process began again until the mound eventually became a great conical form.

Mounds were also used for linear reasons, for literally thousands were constructed as dividing lines between kingdoms or tribes, with some extending for hundreds of miles. They are unstratified and have no deposits in them and are thought to have marked territorial boundaries, since effigy mounds are always found at points where the principal lines intersect one another, thus showing tribal affiliation.[16]

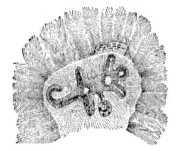

Cat effigy mound. Nadaillac, *Pre-Historic America,* 1893.

Ample evidence supports the premise that much about the mounds are religious in nature. However, after traveling nine hundred miles and examining seventy-six earth-works, and surveying four hundred and forty four mounds, Pidgeon concluded the mound builders in the north, (Illinois, Indiana, and Wisconsin) were of a different religious persuasion than those in the Ohio Valley and southward to Mexico. He observed:

> Many deposits found at the south presenting the known forms of the symbols of ancient idolatry, favors the conclusion that a change of religious belief, or the forms of idolatrous worship occurred among the mound-builders of the south which those at the north did not experience.[18]

This makes perfect sense since the Nephites in New York, who, according to Dragoo, subsequently migrated westward along the lower Great Lakes into Illinois, Ohio, Indiana, and Michigan were not an idolatrous people. Consequently, their antiquities would differ from those of the Lamanites who inhabited the regions more to the south.

The effigy mounds (those that resemble animals and humans) in the lower Great Lakes region fascinate all who gaze upon them. They were a particularly unique form of hieroglyphic writing. All important events such as national events, unions with other tribes, new monarchs, royal marriages etc.,were all recorded in the earth and represented the history of the nation that erected them and the event taking place.

Mounds were erected for every imaginable occasion, even those that represented the union of two or more nations. (Their numbers were diminished by war at times and unions were often necessary.) The hieroglyphic meaning of just such a mound was explained by De-coo-dah and is representative of the many amalgamation mounds found in the region.

Figure 1 represents a triumphant monument, which, according to De-coo-dah, was erected in commemoration of conquest, and in honor of a youthful sovereign who succeeded

Figure 1. Pidgeon. *Traditions of De-Coo-Da.*

Figure 2. Pidgeon. *Traditions of De-Coo-Da.*

to the dominion of the Bear. The fact he is standing on the head of the Bear, indicates "the wisdom of the son in following the counsel of his father and predecessor. The arms extended horizontally, or with equal elevation, records the administration of equal justice to both of the united nations."[19]

Figure 2 "records a reverse of fortune. Here the sovereign, no longer standing erect on the head of the Bear, is seen suspended below it, with drooping arms, and his head pointing to a funeral circle to which is appended the mound of extinction. Nearby is another circle, with a crescent shaped mound, representing the new moon and symbolizing the advent of a new sovereign after the extinction of the race of the vanquished king."[20]

In this way, records Pidgeon, "the ancient mound-builder could read the national prosperity and dignity of his ancestors in the position observed in the construction of their works; while the body, or parts of the body, not only record their name, but also perpetuate the knowledge of the ancient existence of nations long extinct." Thus, according to Pidgeon, "aided by tradition, we read in the hieroglyphical mounds of the earth, the dignity and destiny of nations unknown to written history."

Mounds of so many different shapes and sizes covered the eastern woodlands that many have questioned whether they were built by one people or by many different cultures over an extended period of time. The common consensus is: "The features common to all are elementary and identify them as appertaining to a single grand system."[21]

Not understanding the scriptural account, Thomas, believed otherwise, commenting the only thing these structures had in common was "earth."[22] He continues:

> The thought that once a mighty nation occupied the valley of the Mississippi with its frontier settlements resting on the lake shores and gulf coast, nestling in the valleys of the Appalachian range and skirting the broad plains of the west; a nation with its systems of government and religion, but which has disappeared, leaving behind it no evidence of its glory, power and extent, save these silent, forest-covered remains, has something so fascinating and attractive in it, that once it has taken possession of the mind it warps and biases all its investigations and conclusions.[23]

Thomas also questioned the terms usually used to describe the mounds, such as "Temple Mounds," "Sacred Enclosures," "Altar Mounds," and "Sacrificial Mounds," expressing the opinion that far too little is known of the mounds to classify them with such particular names which would suggest their whole culture revolved around religion. He also criticized those who speculated that just because a few bones were found in the ashes near altars did not automatically ascribe that mound to one that was sacrificial in nature. Although he certainly has a valid point, we must be cautious of being too overly cautious as well. The scriptures shed further light on the matter.

Not only was the law of animal sacrifice an integral part of the Law of Moses, but we learn from the scriptures that at times the Lamanites, who had distorted this sacred rite, had offered many of their Nephite captives up as sacrificial offerings. We learn also that near the end

Altar mound. Squier and Davis, *Ancient Monuments,* 1848.

of the Nephite Era sacrifice was going on regularly among the Lamanites and that many Nephites were being sacrificed in retaliation for Nephite atrocities. Therefore, we can verify that sacrifice did occur in this region by both those who may have observed the sacrificial rites pertaining to the Law of Moses, and those who, under the influence of the Evil One, distorted that sacrificial ordinance to include human sacrifice.

Such practices would not go unnoticed by the Creator, however, for those who lived within the land of promise were under the very strict command to live righteously or be swept away. Thus, we might reasonably speculate that once the Nephites were destroyed, the Lord may have diminished those nations that practiced this unholy ritual. Perhaps he drove them from the country altogether, which might also account for some of the unprecedented savagery and human sacrifice practiced in Central and South America at the time of European contact.

There is still so much to learn of the ancient inhabitants of this and other continents. But, of one thing we can be sure—a great many of the mounds were built for defense. In fact, after careful investigation of the matter, Pidgeon was of the opinion

> The mounds of stone and earth were the last works of the earthen Mound Builders; that they were erected for defense, in anticipation of an assault from a foreign enemy, . . . and by whom they were finally conquered and reduced to the servility which resulted in the total extinction of their nationality.[24]

He was also of the opinion that at least two distinct races of men occupied the territory at different eras, and that both became nationally extinct anterior to the occupation of the present Indian race.

~ ~ ~

Once the Indians were a proud and mighty race, yet by the time of European contact, they appeared to be another race altogether from those mighty builders of the mounds. Speaking of one such tribe, De-coo-dah tells of their degenerate state.

> They were once strong, they are now weak; they were sober and industrious, they are now drunken and lazy; they were wise and honest, now they are foolish and roguish; they have lost their traditions, and know nothing of their fathers; they revel in holy places, and the Great Spirit has forsaken them.[25]

Because the Lord promised their ancient fathers the Lamanites would not be totally swept away along with their Nephite brethren, if, and when, they all became ripe in iniquity, he still could not condone such sinfulness. Therefore, when the time was right, the Lord brought steady streams of Christian pilgrims to America who ultimately scattered and distressed these wayward Lamanites. Thus, one more time the promised land was cleansed of the idolatrous practices of the wicked.

As Pidgeon noted in 1858:

> The last relics of pagan superstition are disappearing from the face of our prosperous and happy country, and the advancing footsteps of civilization are fast leveling to the earth the walls of ancient cities, the sepulchral mounds, and the altars of an idolatrous worship.

Unfortunately, without the written history of those who occupied the eastern woodlands, we must wait upon the Lord's good time for the restoration of ancient records, which will show the true uses of those earthen-works that dot the landscape. For the time being, our only hope of discovering their purpose will be by following closely each new archeological discovery and respecting those traditions handed down by the descendants of those who built them—the Indian Nations of today. Therefore, the traditions handed down by De-coo-dah are worthy of the same consideration we pay to archeological discoveries. In, fact, they appear to be even more enlightening.

~   ~   ~

# Notes

1. Pidgeon, *Traditions of De-Coo-Dah*, 68–69.
2. Silverberg, *Mound Builders*, 109.
3. Pidgeon, *Traditions of De-Coo-Dah*, 57.
4. Silverberg, *Mound Builders*, 111.
5. Pidgeon, *Traditions of De-Coo-Dah*, 103.
6. Ibid., 58.
7. Hanson, *He Walked the Americas*, 59.
8. Ibid.
9. Pidgeon, *Traditions of De-Coo-Dah*, 143.
10. Ibid., 102.
11. Squier and Davis, *Ancient Monuments of the Mississippi Valley*, 68.
12. Silverberg, *Mound Builders*, 52
13. Pidgeon, *Traditions of De-Coo-Dah*, 257.
14. Ibid., 92.
15. Ibid., 100.
16. Ibid., 240.
17. Thomas, *The 12th Annual Report of the Bureau of Ethnology*, 570.
18. Pidgeon, *Traditions of De-Coo-Dah*, 203.
19. Ibid., 209.
20. Ibid., 211.
21. Squier and Davis, *Ancient Monuments of the Mississippi Valley*, 301.
22. Thomas, *The 12th Annual Report of the Bureau of Ethnology*, 602.
23. Ibid., 605.
24. Pidgeon, *Traditions of De-Coo-Dah*, 278.
25. Ibid., 142.

Angel Moroni. Courtesy The Church of
Jesus Christ of Latter-day Saints.

# Final Thoughts

It was in this ever expanding atmosphere of speculation and conjecture regarding the builders of the mounds that Joseph Smith and his seemingly fantastic tale of golden plates first came upon the scene. Joseph loved the mystery surrounding the mounds and often pondered the very same questions many others had. But his life was about to change forever, and, unbeknownst to him, the answers to the long debated questions as to the origin of the Mound Builders was about to be revealed.

In 1823, a heavenly messenger appeared to Joseph Smith and informed him of sacred tablets which had been hidden up in the earth by the ancient inhabitants of the area. He was told the time had come for these records to come forth. Beyond giving an historical record of the region, they were to act as a second witness of Jesus Christ; that same Jesus Christ who had visited the ancient inhabitants of America after his death and resurrection. That awesome occasion began as follows:

199

"On the evening of the . . . twenty first of September [1823] . . . I betook myself to prayer and supplication to Almighty God. . . .

"While I was thus in the act of calling upon God, I discovered a light appearing in my room, which continued to increase until the room was lighter than at noonday, when immediately a personage appeared at my bedside, standing in the air, for his feet did not touch the floor.

"He had on a loose robe of most exquisite whiteness. It was a whiteness beyond anything earthly I had ever seen; nor do I believe that any earthly thing could be made to appear so exceedingly white and brilliant. His hands were naked, and his arms also, a little above the wrists; so, also, were his feet naked, as were his legs, a little above the ankles. His head and neck were also bare. I could discover that he had no other clothing on but this robe, as it was open, so that I could see into his bosom.

"Not only was his robe exceedingly white, but his whole person was glorious beyond description, and his countenance truly like lightening. The room was exceedingly light, but not so very bright as immediately around his person. When I first looked upon him, I was afraid; but the fear soon left me.

"He called me by name, and said unto me that he was a messenger sent from the presence of God to me, and that his name was Moroni; that God had a work for me to do; and that my name should be had for good and evil among all nations, kindreds, and tongues, or that it should be both good and evil spoken of among all people.

"He said there was a book deposited, written upon gold plates, giving an account of the former inhabitants of this continent, and the source from whence they sprang. He also said that the fulness of the everlasting gospel was contained in it, as delivered by the Savior to the ancient inhabitants;

"Also, that there were two stones in silver bows—and these stones, fastened to a breastplate, constituted what is called the Urim and Thummim-deposited with the plates; and the possession and use of these stones were what constituted Seers in ancient or former times; and that God had prepared them for the purpose of translating the book. . . .

After this communication, I saw the light in the room begin to gather immediately around the person of him who had been speaking to me, and it continued to do so, until the room was again left dark, except just around him, when instantly I saw, as it were, a conduit open right up into heaven, and he ascended until he entirely disappeared, and the room was left as it had been before this heavenly light had made its appearance.[1]

### Orson Pratt recaps more of that message:

He was also informed that he was called and chosen to be an instrument in the hands of God to bring about some of his marvelous purposes in this glorious dispensation. It was also made manifest to him, that the "American Indians" were a remnant of Israel; that when they first emigrated to America they were an enlightened people, possessing a knowledge of the true God, enjoying his favor; and peculiar blessings from his hand; that the prophets, and inspired writers among them, were required to keep a sacred history of the most important events transpiring among them: which history was handed down for many generations, till at length they fell into great wickedness: the most part of them were destroyed, and the record, by commandment of God to one of the last prophets among them,) were safely deposited, to preserve them from the hands of the wicked, who sought to destroy them. He was informed, that these records contained many sacred revelations pertaining to the gospel of the kingdom, as well as prophecies relating to the great events of the last days; and to fulfill his promises to the ancients, who wrote the records, and to accomplish his purposes in the restitution of their children, etc.[2]

Thus, a series of events began which were destined to prepare the way for the gathering of Israel from the four corners of the earth in preparation for the Lord's triumphant return.

Joseph ultimately retrieved the Golden Plates from the Hill Cumorah in New York State in 1827, where they had been buried and preserved by the hand of the Lord for over fourteen hundred years. They were subsequently translated by divine means in preparation for the restitution of all things. The translated work is now known as the Book of Mormon, named after the ancient prophet who abridged them.

This body of scripture is both a spiritual and historical record of the inhabitants of what the scriptures refer to as the promised land; a territory near the present day Hill Cumorah in New York State where the plates were first deposited by Moroni, the son of Mormon, after the destruction of his people around the year A.D. 400. From its pages we learn of two civilizations which had their origins in the Old World during periods of great wickedness. They were ultimately separated from their people and were led by the hand of the Lord across the great deep to a new land at two distinct periods of time. The Jaredites were led away from the Tower of Babel shortly after the Universal Flood, and the Mulekites and Nephites were led away long after Israel had been established as a nation; the Mulekites during the reign of King Zedekiah and the Nephites, under the direction of Lehi, being led away just prior to the destruction of Jerusalem six hundred years before the birth of Christ.

These ancient tablets reveal that two great nations flourished in America as a result of these immigrations; the Jaredite nation for about thirteen hundred years and the Nephites for nine hundred. Unfortunately, each nation was fraught with warfare and dissensions of various kinds and each eventually fought battles of near complete annihilation around the Hill Cumorah at the close of their respective eras. Sadly, the Jaredites, the most ancient of the two civilizations, completely exterminated one another. The inhabitants of the second civilization, the Nephites, met the same fatal end in a horrific battle around the Hill Cumorah in A.D. 400. But, a remnant of that civilization, the victorious Lamanites, were permitted to remain in the land in fulfillment of promises made to earlier prophets in their behalf.

Evidence heretofore given, indicates the Mound Builders of the Woodland Epoch were none other than the Nephites and the Lamanites of the Book of Mormon. The numerous pieces of the puzzle, both scriptural and archeological, have been brought together in this body of work to produce a picture complete enough to support the premise that the Nephite Nation and the Mound Builders were one and the same. Thus, those theories which continued to pit one school of thought against the other over the years, with one suggesting a lost race of superior beings built the mounds and the other that the Indians had done so, could have easily been reconciled with the inclusion of just one common denominator—the history contained within the Book of Mormon.

~ ~ ~

In light of the spirit of skepticism that prevailed in the region during the time Joseph was entrusted with the Golden Plates, it is no wonder his sacred experience was met with such disdain. So many stories of the discovery of ancient tablets and their supposed authenticity had surfaced over the years that many people lost their enthusiasm for them. Even so, the story of the Golden Plates and the young Prophet Joseph Smith caused quite a stir among the people. And, while many believed, others set out to discount his story in any way they could.

The various theories about the origin of the mounds and the numerous antiquities found in the area, including those entrusted to Joseph, were passed back and forth between merchants and customers, writers and readers, politicians, scientists, archeologists, and the general population as a whole for decades. Unfortunately, as anti-Mormon sentiment began to rear its ugly head, even more impressive artifacts were relegated to the status of fakes or to those of European origins, and far too many were simply discarded.

With the passing of time, however, more accurate scientific methods of forgery detection are proving that many of those once thought to be fakes are actually genuine. Thus, more and more pieces of the puzzle are coming to light, and, as each puzzle piece falls into place with the next, the authenticity of the Book of Mormon is verified further.

Even so, while the Savior personably ministered to his flock in the meridian of time, it will be by the powerful influence of the Holy Ghost that the Gentiles of the Latter-days will be converted.

> And they understood me not that I said they shall hear my voice; and they understood me not that the Gentiles should not at any time hear my voice-that I should not manifest myself unto them save it were by the Holy Ghost. (3 Ne. 15:23)

As numerous converts will gladly testify, physical verification has not been necessary to this generation. Those who read and believe have been touched by the Spirit and will move heaven and earth to join the fold. Those who don't, will not. Moreover, those who use every method to disprove this evidence or that, are on a mission going nowhere. The Spirit of the Holy Ghost speaks to the heart, and those with real intent and a thirst for knowledge will embrace the truth whenever and wherever it is presented to them.

The time is short, and the gathering must continue before the field is burned in preparation for the Second Advent of the Savior. There is still much work to do, and those who teach the gospel among the nations of the world will continue to present the Book of Mormon to their contacts. The message of hope and salvation contained within its pages, and the powerful impact of the Holy Ghost upon the hearts of those who seek for truth, is all that is needed to propel the righteous onward toward life eternal.

~ ~ ~

The scriptures inform us that other records are yet to come forth; records written by numerous prophets throughout the ages, which have been hid from the eye of all the world until such time as the Lord tries the faith of his people and finds them worthy of further light and knowledge.

> Behold, I was about to write them, all which were engraven upon the plates of Nephi, but the Lord forbade it, saying: I will try the faith of my people.
>
> Therefore I, Mormon, do write the things which have been commanded me of the Lord. And now I, Mormon, make an end of my sayings, and proceed to write the things which have been commanded me. (3 Ne. 26:11–12)

Even without physical verification, the Savior's sheep will hear his voice wherever they are, whether in the north or south or east or west, for the Holy Ghost will manifests the truth of it to them. And, after walking by faith for a time, further light and knowledge will be imparted. Perhaps that time is nearing, for the signs are present everywhere, and the evidence is compelling that those whose history is contained in the Book of Mormon lived in the promised land of America, with other colonies scattered throughout the world.

The end times are nearing and the wheat and the tares are clearly being separated. The purposes of the Lord in gathering his flock from the four corners of the earth has begun and will continue to roll forth until all the scattered of Israel have been safely gathered into the fold. Moreover, all the honest in heart are invited to join them and be partakers of those glorious blessings reserved for the honest in heart, for not one soul who loves the Savior and yearns for salvation will ever be lost. Amen.

~ ~ ~

## Notes

1. "Testimony of the Prophet Joseph Smith," Book of Mormon.
2. Orson Pratt, in Jessee, *Papers of Joseph Smith*, 1:393.

# Bibliography

Adair, James. *Adair's History of the American Indians.* Ed. Samuel Cole Williams. 1775. Johnson City, Tenn.: Watauga Press, 1930. Reprint. New York: Promontary Press, [1974].

Baldwin, John D. *Ancient America in Notes on American Archaeology.* New York: Harper and Brothers, 1872.

Caroli, Kenneth. "Wisconsin's Underwater Discoveries and the Outside World in Prehistory." *Ancient American Magazine,* no. 33 (2000): 12–14.

Conant, A. J. *Foot-prints of Vanished Races in the Mississippi Valley.* St. Louis: Chancy R. Barnes, 1879.

Dragoo, Don W. "The Development of Adena Culture and Its Role in the Formation of Ohio Hopewell." In *Hopewellian Studies,* ed. Joseph R. Caldwell and Robert L. Hall, 1–34. Illinois State Museum Scientific Papers, vol. 12. Springfield, Ill.: Printed by Authority of the State of Illinois, 1964.

———. *Mounds for the Dead: An Analysis of the Adena Culture.* Annals of Carnegie Museum, vol. 37. Pittsburgh: By authority of the Board of Trustees of the Carnegie Institute, [1963].

DuTemple, Octave J. "Prehistory's Greatest Mystery: Copper Mines of Ancient Michigan." *Ancient American Magazine,* no. 35 (2000): 8–13.

Foster, J. W. *Pre-historic Races of the United States.* Chicago: S. C. Griggs and Co.; London: Trubner and Co., 1873.

Godfrey, Kenneth W. "The Zelph Story." *BYU Studies* 29 (spring 1989): 31–56.

Grimes, Jim. "Who Mined Great Lakes' Copper 4,000 Years Ago." *Ancient American Magazine,* no. 35 (2000): 28–30.

Hansen, L. Taylor. *He Walked the Americas.* Amherst, Wisc.: Legend Press, 1963.

Hunter, Milton R., to Ellis Clarke Soper, January 20, 1965. Paul Chessman Papers, MSS 2049, series F, box 80, fld. 3. L. Tom Perry Special Collections Library, Harold B. Lee Library, Brigham Young University, Provo, Utah.

Jessee, Dean C., ed. *The Papers of Joseph Smith.* 2 vols. Salt Lake City: Deseret Book, 1989–92.

———, ed. and comp. *The Personal Writings of Joseph Smith.* Salt Lake City: Deseret Book, 1984.

Korp, Maureen. *The Sacred Geography of the American Mound Builders.* Native American Studies, vol. 2. Lewiston, N.Y.: Edwin Mcllen Press, 1990.

McGavin, E. Cecil, and Willard Bean. *The Geography of the Book of Mormon.* Salt Lake City: Bookcraft, 1949.

MacLean, J. P. *The Mound Builders.* Cincinnati: Robert Clark and Co., 1879.

Mertz, Henriette. *Atlantis.* Chicago: by the author, 1996.

———. *The Mystic Symbol: Mark of the Michigan Mound Builders.* Gaithersburg, Md.: Global Books.

*Mound Builders & Cliff Dwellers.* Alexandria, Va.: Time-Life Books, 1992.

Nadaillac, Marquis de. *Pre-Historic America.* New York: G. P. Putnam's Sons, 1893.

O'Brien, T. J. *Pale Gods and Feathered Serpents.* Bountiful, Utah: Horizon Publishers, 1997.

Pidgeon, William. *Traditions of De-Coo-Dah.* New York: Horace Thayer, 1858.

Priest, Josiah. *American Antiquities and Discoveries of the West.* Albany, N.Y.: Hoffman and White, 1883.

———. *Wonders of Nature and Providence.* Albany, N.Y.: By the author, 1825.

Prufer, Olaf H. "The Hopewell Complex of Ohio." In *Hopewellian Studies,* ed. Joseph R. Caldwell and Robert L. Hall, 35–83. Illinois State Museum Scientific Papers, vol. 12. Springfield, Ill.: Printed by Authority of the State of Illinois, 1964.

Putnam, Charles E. *Vindication of the Authenticity of the Elephant Pipes and Inscribed Tablets.* Davenport, Iowa: Davenport Academy of Natural Sciences, 1885.

Roberts, B. H. *New Witness for God.* 3 vols. Salt Lake City: Deseret News, 1909–11.

Scherz, James. "The Stone Face at Mummy Mountain." *Ancient American Magazine,* no. 32 (2000): 2–4.

Shaffer, Lynda Norene. *Native Americans before 1492.* Armonk, N.Y.: M. E. Sharp, 1992.

Silverburg, Robert. *The Mound Builders.* Athens: Ohio University Press, 1970.

Squire, E. G. *Antiquities of the State of New York.* Buffalo, N.Y.: Geo. H. Derby and Co., 1851.

Squire, E. G., and E. H. Davies. *Ancient Monuments of the Mississippi Valley.* Smithsonian Contributions to Knowledge. New York: Bartlett and Welford; Cincinnati: J. A. and U. P. James, 1847.

Talmage, James E. "The Michigan Relics: A Story of Forgery and Deception." *Deseret Museum Bulletin,* n.s., no. 2, (September 16, 1911). Church Archives, Family and Church History Department, The Church of Jesus Christ of Latter-day Saints, Salt Lake City.

Thomas, Cyrus. *12th Annual Report of the Bureau of Ethnology.* Washington, D.C., 1890–91.

Turner, O. *Pioneer History of the Holland Purchase of Western New York.* Buffalo, N.Y.: Jewett Thomas and Co., 1849.

# CEDAR FORT, INCORPORATED
## Order Form

Name:_____

Address: _____

City: _____ State: _____ Zip: _____

Phone: (    ) _____ Daytime phone: (    ) _____

### *Lost Tribes of the Book of Mormon*

Quantity: _____ @ $13.95 each:       _____

plus $3.49 shipping & handling for the first book:       _____

(add 99¢ shipping for each additional book)

Utah residents add 6.25% for state sales tax:       _____

                    TOTAL:       _____

Bulk purchasing, shipping and handling quotes available upon request.

Please make check or money order payable to:
Cedar Fort, Incorporated.

Mail this form and payment to:
Cedar Fort, Inc.
925 North Main St.
Springville, UT 84663

You can also order on our website **www.cedarfort.com**
or e-mail us at sales@cedarfort.com or call 1-800-SKYBOOK